HOMEFRONT COOKING

HOMEFRONT COOKING

RECIPES, WIT, AND WISDOM FROM AMERICAN VETERANS AND THEIR LOVED ONES

By
Tracey Enerson Wood
with
Beth Guidry Riffle,
Carol Van Drie, and many more

Skyhorse Publishing

Skyhorse Publishing books may be purchased in bulk at special discounts for sales promotion, corporate gifts, fund-raising, or educational purposes. Special editions can also be created to specifications. For details, contact the Special Sales Department, Skyhorse Publishing, 307 West 36th Street, 11th Floor, New York, NY 10018 or info@skyhorsepublishing.com.

Skyhorse® and Skyhorse Publishing® are registered trademarks of Skyhorse Publishing, Inc.®, a Delaware corporation.

Visit our website at www.skyhorsepublishing.com.

10 9 8 7 6 5 4 3 2 1

Library of Congress Cataloging-in-Publication Data is available on file.

Cover design by Mona Lin
Cover photo: iStockphoto

Print ISBN: 978-1-5107-2870-7
Ebook ISBN: 978-1-5107-2871-4

Printed in the United States of America

DEDICATION

My great uncle, Timothy Cusack, fought in World War I. My great-grandparents saved the letters he wrote from the front, and they have been passed down through the generations. Sweet and wistful, they shed light on what was important to a young man, torn from his home and family, and thrown into the horror of war.

The themes in his letters resonate today as much as they did then. Love of family. A sense of duty to country. A longing for home. A need to communicate, to know how loved ones are doing, and to assure his family of his well-being. Private Cusack begged for letters from home; it seemed that knowing the details of their daily lives kept him going.

And food. Although not a major preoccupation, most letters mention the availability, the cost, and the enjoyment of food. He described a great feast, with beer, wine, and a roast pig. He complained about the cost of fresh eggs and other delicacies, but delighted in eating them. This is not so different from today.

Private Timothy Cusack did not make it back to the family he wrote to with so much love. He was buried in France on November 8, 1918, just three days before the Great War was over.

This book is dedicated to all who have served, in peace and in war, whether at the front lines of a foreign conflict, or saving tin foil and eating blueberries for dinner on the homefront.

May every meal be a celebration of life and love.

—*Tracey Enerson Wood*
Daughter, daughter-in-law, sister, wife, mother, mother-in-law,
niece, cousin, and friend of veterans
St. Petersburg, Florida

Table of Contents

PART IV: MORE DIMES THAN DOLLARS

PART V: POT LUCK

PART VI: COMFORT FOODS

FINAL THOUGHTS

PART I: REVEILLE
Breakfast and Other Eye-Openers

A Promise Kept

It is June, 1944, two days after D-day. Bernardo Doganiero, a handsome American soldier, has arrived in Rennes, France, with the 127th General Hospital. The unit has been tasked with opening a military hospital on the site of the former German medical facility on Rue de l'Hotel Dieu. As he walks the several blocks from the barracks to the hospital, he notices a scrawny little girl watching him. She has dark eyes, brown curls, and clothes two sizes too small. Struck by the intensity of her stare, he gives her a smile. She smiles back, shyly.

Thus begins a beautiful friendship that will span an ocean and a generation.

From that day on, Bernardo finds the little girl waiting for him on the corner every morning. She follows him to the hospital, chattering in French. At the end of his shift, she is waiting by the hospital gate to walk him home. He teaches her a few English words, she helps him expand his French vocabulary, and, along with some exaggerated pantomiming, they manage to overcome the language barrier. He learns that her name is Jacqueline Halna, and she is eleven years old. Her father, a pilot for the French Resistance, has been lost in battle. She and her mother live in a cramped apartment on Rue Noel du Fail.

Having managed to survive many years of brutal Nazi occupation, Jacqueline, along with the rest of the Rennes population, is overjoyed with the arrival of the Americans. She seems in awe of the men and women who work at the hospital, and her plucky personality and resilient nature endear her to them. She soon becomes the sweetheart of the 127th General, but Bernardo remains her favorite, and their friendship continues throughout his deployment in Rennes. He senses that he's become a surrogate father for Jacqueline and begins to worry about how she'll react when the unit is reassigned.

The dreaded day finally arrives on January 1, 1945. Sleet is falling as Bernardo and his unit pack the trucks that will carry them to the city of Nancy to set up another hospital. Hearing a familiar voice calling his name, Bernardo turns to see Jacqueline shivering in the cold. She wears only a thin sweater over her dress. With tears in her eyes, she presents him with two gifts—a loaf of bread baked by her mother and a book given to her by her father. Inscribed on the first page in Jacqueline's child-like script, are the words "*Souvenir de Jacqueline Halna, A mi cher ami Bernardo*" ("A remembrance of Jacqueline Halna, To my dear friend Bernardo").

Realizing the tremendous sacrifice those gifts represent coming from someone with so little, Bernardo takes off his heavy woolen coat and wraps it around her, telling her this is his gift. Then, with a hug, he makes her a promise—that if he ever has a daughter, he will name her Jacqueline.

This was the only war story my father was willing to share. I heard it countless times over the years, and it became part of our family lore. But no matter how many times he told it, he always ended it the same way. He'd smile at me, often with misty eyes that seemed to look back through time, and say, "You're living proof that I've kept my promise."

SFC Bernardo Minniti with Jacqueline Halna, December, 1944.

French Bread

Yield: 1 loaf

Ingredients:

¼-oz. pkg. active dry yeast
1 c. warm water
2 tbsp. sugar
2 tbsp. corn oil
1½ tsp. salt
3–3½ c. all-purpose flour
Cornmeal
1 egg white
1 tsp. cold water

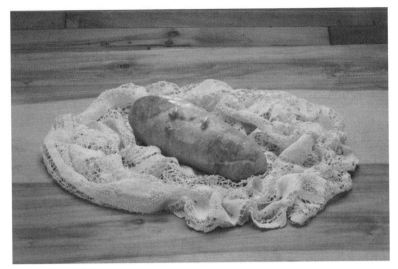

Photo by Steve Dean Photography

Directions:

In a large bowl, dissolve yeast in warm water.

Add the sugar, oil, salt, and 2 cups flour. Beat until blended. Stir in enough of the remaining flour to form a stiff dough.

Turn onto a floured board. Knead about 6–8 minutes until smooth. Place in a greased bowl, turning once. Cover and let rise in a warm place until doubled (about an hour.) Punch dough down; return to bowl. Cover and let rise for 30 more minutes.

Punch dough down. Turn onto floured board. Roll into a 16-in. loaf with tapered ends.

Transfer loaf to greased baking sheet which has been sprinkled with cornmeal. Cover and let rise until doubled (about 30 minutes).

Beat egg white and cold water; brush over dough. Cut diagonal slits across top of loaf.

Bake at 375°F for 25–30 minutes or until golden brown.

Cool on a wire rack.

—*Jackie Minniti*
Award-winning author of Jacqueline *and* Project June Bug

Busy Family Breakfast

During deployments, I am usually the only adult in my house, and I am responsible for my four young children. This can make deployment mealtimes a frustrating challenge. Breakfast is especially hard, since I am barely awake and functional, but the kids all start their day at full energy and volume levels. I quickly realized there was no time to prepare breakfast for myself, when I was simultaneously pouring four bowls of cereal and cleaning spilled juice off the floor.

Deployment mornings go much more smoothly when I make my breakfast the night before. During our last deployment, this was one of my go-to meals. I can cook when the kids are in bed, and make a big batch of these breakfast quesadillas to put in the fridge or freezer. It is easy to warm them up in the morning. I sometimes ate them as a healthy lunch, too! Having a batch of these beauties cooked and ready made me feel like I had money in the bank, and I knew I wouldn't be running on empty all day.

When my husband returned from deployment, I introduced him to this recipe, and he loves it too! The combination of eggs, spinach, garlic, beans, and white cheddar is a delightful way to wake up and start your day.

Photo by Steve Dean Photography

Breakfast Quesadillas

Serves 8

Ingredients:

8 eggs
Splash of milk (optional)
1 tbsp. olive oil
10-oz. bag of fresh spinach, washed
2 cloves garlic, minced

Salt and pepper to taste
15-oz. can white navy beans, rinsed
8 medium wheat tortillas
8 oz. white cheddar cheese, shredded

Directions:

Beat 8 eggs in a bowl. Add a splash of milk for fluffier consistency, if desired.

Put olive oil in a large saucepan on medium heat. Add the bag of spinach and allow it to slowly wilt down, stirring occasionally, about 3 minutes.

When it is cooked, add the garlic, salt, pepper, and beans. Immediately add the beaten eggs to the pan, and stir constantly to make a scrambled egg mixture. Once the eggs are fully cooked, remove the saucepan from heat, and allow to cool slightly.

Place a heaping spoonful of egg and bean mixture, and 1 ounce of shredded cheese about ⅓ the distance from the edge on each tortilla. Fold the short edge over the filling, then roll up the rest of the way, forming a cylinder shape, with the open edge down.

Wrap each quesadilla in plastic wrap or foil.

They can be stored in the fridge for a few days, or the freezer for months. Defrost in the microwave, or place in the fridge overnight.

When ready to eat, place a defrosted quesadilla in a small saucepan sprayed with nonstick spray. Heat on medium heat for a few moments on each side, until lightly brown and crisp.

Enjoy!

—Lizann Lightfoot
Creator of The Seasoned Spouse blog: www.SeasonedSpouse.com

In Search of the Perfect Bagel

Growing up in Northern New Jersey, there were several dietary staples I was accustomed to. After I married a military guy, the Army promptly whisked us away to all corners of the country and world, and I was rather shocked to find these familiar things were not available. At least, they weren't available to my liking. Pizza, for example, although the quality has greatly improved lately, is always best in New York or New Jersey. And maybe Italy, but the Army never saw fit to station us there. Sorry Chicagoans, that deep-dish stuff you eat is tasty, but not pizza.

Another is Taylor Ham, (or Pork Roll for the Central to South Jersey folks). I can now find it in Florida, but for years I craved it as the Army insisted on stationing us outside the official Taylor Ham distribution area (basically New Jersey).

And oh, the bagels. I like a good New York bagel. Chewy, with a light crust. Aromatic, and so fresh, the malty, yeasty aroma nearly causes me to swoon when I cut into it. Savory, please. Raisins and cinnamon should be banned by law from coming within twenty feet of a bagel. Yes, I'm opinionated. I did warn you I'm from New Jersey.

Alas, in the twenty states and two countries in which I have lived post-marriage, the perfect bagel cannot be found. The sorry excuses for them, even in so-called "bagel shops," are edible only if you have a vivid enough imagination to convince yourself they are.

So, after years of experimentation, and perhaps a thousand doughy pucks of gustatory displeasure, I can now make a decent bagel. It is a time-consuming, messy project, with ingredients I have to order on the Internet, but still worth it.

New York Bagels

Makes 8 bagels

Ingredients:

1½ tsp. active dry yeast

1 tbsp. barley malt powder (diastatic preferred) or barley malt syrup

1¼ c. lukewarm water (about 100°F)

1 tbsp. kosher salt

4 c. bread flour (I like King Arthur brand)

1 tbsp. wheat gluten

Poaching liquid:

3 qts. water

1 tbsp. barley malt

1 tbsp. baking soda

1 tsp. kosher salt

Optional:

1 egg, beaten

Poppy or sesame seeds, garlic or onion flakes

Directions:

Stir yeast and malt powder into lukewarm water. Let stand 5–10 minutes until it foams. (If you don't get some foam, your yeast is no good.) Add salt.

Sift together flour and gluten in large mixing bowl. Add 1 cup of the yeast/water mixture.

If using a stand mixer, use dough hook at low speed for 3 minutes. Dough should form a stiff, coarse ball.

If there is flour left over that won't mix in, add water/yeast, a few drops at a time, until all flour is mixed in. Let rest about 5 minutes.

Continue mixing at slow speed until you have a smooth, stiff ball, about 8–10 minutes. Cut dough into 8 equal pieces.

Shape each piece into a ball, then on a clean, dry surface roll into logs about 8–10 inches long.

Flatten each end of log slightly, then lightly moisten ends and press together to make a ring.

Set aside at room temperature to rise, about 1 hour, or refrigerate overnight, then take out 1–1½ hours before ready to continue. This method results in the tastiest result.

Combine all poaching liquid ingredients and bring to a boil in a large pot.

continued on page 10

Preheat oven to 450°F. (Optional: preheat baking stone in center of oven. May also use a cookie sheet with Silpat liner.)

Test the dough by placing one ring in a bowl of cold water—if it floats, they are all ready. When a ring passes the float test, boil them in your poaching liquid, 3–4 at a time, for one minute. Turn, boil 30 more seconds, then remove to draining rack.

If desired, brush with a beaten egg, and sprinkle on toppings, such as poppy seeds, sesame seeds, onion, or garlic flakes.

Slide rings onto baking stone or cookie sheet with liner and bake for 8 minutes.

Turn baking stone around and bake for another 8 minutes, or until golden brown.

—Tracey Enerson Wood
St. Petersburg, FL

Bagel and Lox Benedict

Serves 8

Ingredients:

Cream cheese fondue:
1½ c. half-and-half
1 c. cream cheese
¼ tsp. fresh thyme
¼ tsp. Old Bay Seasoning
   (+ more to garnish)
Salt and pepper to taste
6 c. boiling water with ¼ c. white vinegar

8 eggs
4 bagels (everything bagels suggested), split
   and toasted
Fresh smoked salmon (from your local
   market)
3-oz. jar of capers
1 red onion, sliced
Microgreens for garnish

Directions:

Heat half-and-half. Add cream cheese and other fondue ingredients. Mix well, until smooth and creamy.

Poaching eggs:

Heat water and vinegar to a medium boil.

Stir in one direction with sauce spoon, then carefully drop an egg into the center of the whirlpool. The swirling water will help prevent the white from "feathering," or spreading out in the pan. Allow to cook for 5 minutes, then remove egg from water with perforated spoon.

Arrange a toasted bagel half on your plate. Add the smoked salmon, poached egg, cream cheese fondue, capers, and onion slices. Garnish with a pinch of Old Bay seasoning and microgreens.

—David Enerson
Jacksonville, FL

Miracle in the South Pacific

In 1943, my father, Henry Zupa, answered the call of duty to serve our country in World War II. After basic training in the states, he was shipped to the South Pacific, landing first in New Zealand for vigorous combat training. Knowing he was soon to be transported to another island to face battle, he was a brave and determined soldier, but as an eighteen-year-old in a foreign land, he was gripped with homesickness.

Dad recounts how, while exploring the town of Auckland, New Zealand, on a weekend pass from the Army camp, he experienced an encounter that could be called a coincidence. Dad likes to call it a miracle.

"I was looking for the zoo," Dad remembers. "I wanted to try to relax before we were shipped out again." After walking for some time through the

PFC Henry Zupa.

town, he lost his way. "I saw an older gentleman standing on the corner, and I approached him to ask for directions." The stranger was pleasant and friendly, giving my father some tips on visiting the local spots. As they chatted, Dad noticed the man had a distinct European accent. "I asked him where he was originally from," Dad recalls. "When he told me Orebic, Yugoslavia, I almost fell over!" Dad's father was born and raised in Orebic. "As it turned out, this man, John, was raised by my grandparents as a foster child. So, there I stood, 9,000 miles from home, with a stranger who turned out to be my 'uncle'!"

Needless to say, Dad spent the weekend with John and his family at their home. Over a delicious feast of roast lamb with mint jelly (a New Zealand favorite), and all the fixings, John shared stories of life in Croatia (formerly Yugoslavia), what it was like growing up in the Zupa household, and the adventures of moving from Europe to settle in New Zealand. My grandfather had immigrated to the United States at an early age, and my dad never had the opportunity to meet his grandparents.

Dad was treated to remarkable tales about a part of the family he had never known, all while being surrounded by his new-found family, at a time when he especially needed the comfort of loved ones. A miracle, I'd say.

To celebrate our Croatian heritage, we love to make Palacinke, a wonderful, easy dessert that the kids love!

Henry Zupa received N.J. Distinguished Service Award, accompanied by daughters: Paula Gruja, Michele Cable, Margo Hess, and Renee Zupa.

Palacinke (Croatian Crepes)

Yields approximately 12 crepes

Ingredients:

3 eggs
1 c. milk
⅓ c. club soda
1 c. flour
3 tbsp. sugar
Pinch of salt

1 tsp. vanilla
Butter or oil for pan
For filling: your choice of jam, Nutella, or
    cinnamon-sugar butter.
Powdered sugar

Directions:

Beat eggs and milk in a mixing bowl. Add the club soda and stir.

In a separate bowl, mix flour, sugar, and salt until well blended, then add to the egg mixture. Add vanilla. The batter will have a very thin consistency.

Heat an 8-inch pan over medium-high heat and add butter or cooking oil to grease the pan. Pour a small amount of batter into pan (keep it thin—think crepe, not pancake!), and tilt to spread evenly. Cook for about 2 minutes, then flip and cook the other side until lightly brown.

Stack the finished crepes with wax paper in between each until ready to fill.

When the crepes are done, spread with either jam, Nutella, or a mix of cinnamon and sugar in a little butter.

Roll the crepe into a cylinder and dust with powdered sugar. Serve warm or at room temperature.

—Michele Cable
Daughter of Henry M. Zupa, WWII veteran
Mother of two active-duty Air Force sons, Alexander and Henry

Cracked Eggs

My dad insisted he ate little more than watery powdered eggs for breakfast during his three years in the Army, so he always cooked eggs sunny-side up, basted with bacon grease.

Dad, in the tradition of his Irish ancestors, was a great storyteller, slipping into a brogue as effortlessly as the wind blows across the fair green isle. His stories had a moral and a bit of humor, but as children we were transfixed by the waggle of his bushy eyebrows, the rising rosiness of his cheeks and the characters he brought to life, each with their own accent and gestures.

One of his favorite stories concerned an incident when he was about ten years old. It was the height of the Depression, and his parents, like so many others, struggled to feed their family. My dad, the eldest of four children, did his part by working in the vegetable garden, feeding his baby sister, and running errands.

"Bubsy, go next door to the Steinberg's and get some eggs," his mother said, handing him a precious dime.

"How many should I get?" he asked, knowing a dozen cost fifteen cents.

"We need a dozen for supper and breakfast tomorrow."

"Yes, Mommy." Confused, he hesitated, squeezing the dime in the palm of his hand.

"Ask for the cracked ones." Handing him an empty wicker basket, his mom nudged him out the door.

The Steinbergs were an elderly couple, who made ends meet by keeping chickens in their basement. Dad both feared and admired his stern neighbors, having watched Mr. Steinberg whack the head off a chicken with a single swipe of a hatchet.

In a pitch-perfect Yiddish accent, Dad quoted Mrs. Steinberg answering the door that day. "Robert Enerson, you are a sight. Have you brought back my cookie tin?"

"No ma'am." He stared at his scuffed brown shoes.

"Then what is it, boy? I haven't all day."

He opened his palm and held out the dime. "I'd like some eggs, please."

"Come in, young man." She took the basket and the dime. "You want eight eggs, then?"

"A dozen please." He looked up at her raised eyebrows, quickly adding, "but only the cracked ones."

"Sit yourself down." She waved him toward a sofa as she headed to a door that led to the basement.

"Saul!" she shouted down the stairs. "Young Robert needs a dozen cracked eggs."

"I haven't any cracked ones." Came the distant reply.

"I said I need a dozen cracked eggs," she said, a bit more sternly.

Dad got off the sofa and crept closer to hear.

"I have no cracked eggs, I tell you."

Sotto voce, she replied, "Then crack some."

—Tracey Enerson Wood
St. Petersburg, FL

Life After Retirement

This recipe is wonderful to serve on cold fall or winter mornings, after your family or guests have been outside hiking, riding horses, or sledding. We retired from the Army in 1984 and moved to a beautiful Pennsylvania farm. Our daughter Molly was thrilled that our farm had a working barn, and her horse and other horses we accumulated, were quite cozy there. The family soon discovered the sport of fox hunting, and joined a hunt club nearby.

On cold fall mornings, after hunting with the hounds, the riders would often come back to our farmhouse for a hearty breakfast. As the riders came through the front door, they always exclaimed when they caught the whiff of cinnamon and hot apples drifting out from the kitchen!

My daughter, Molly, is on the white horse, and her father, Bill, is on the bay.

Our barn, 2016.

Apple-Raisin French Toast

Serves 12

Ingredients:

1 c. brown sugar

½ c. butter (1 stick)

2 tbsp. corn syrup

4 large tart apples, peeled, sliced

1 loaf raisin bread with crust, cubed

12 eggs (may use half Egg Beaters)

1½ c. half-and-half

1 tsp. vanilla or almond extract

2 tsp. cinnamon

Photo by Steve Dean Photography

Directions:

Pour sugar, butter, and corn syrup into 12 x 15-inch glass baking dish. Microwave until melted, and stir to blend.

Spread apples over syrup mixture, and then spread the bread cubes.

In a blender, combine eggs, half-and-half, and vanilla or almond extract; blend well. Pour over bread. Sprinkle with cinnamon. Cover and refrigerate for 1 hour or overnight.

Bake at 350°F, uncovered, for 50 minutes.

You may serve with warm maple syrup, but you don't need it!

—Alicelee Edgerton
Family member, Retired Army
Carlisle, PA

Fat Joe

When I was at the Naval Academy and again on my first aircraft carrier, I noticed that some sandwiches, entrees, or meals were named after people. "Cup of Joe," which most people know is coffee, was named after a Secretary of the Navy who banned alcohol on ships (so that surly sailors now drinking coffee would refer to it as his drink). However, sometimes food items were named with much more ease. I cannot recall what the meal was, but on my carrier I noted that one thing was named for a guy who simply ordered something a lot.

Seeing my opportunity, I decided that I would order something totally ridiculous, and noteworthy, yet tasty. I would order it enough, that maybe it would be named after me.

Aviators need almost as much night flying time as day so that they can maintain their night proficiency. War often requires 24-hour operations so you have to be ready for both day and night. Because of that, the flight schedule requires a late wakeup and a late workday, typically 10:00 a.m. to midnight on a "cruise" (not the Carnival type, mind you). Because of this, Aviators typically eat lunch, dinner, and "midrats" (midnight rations) for their three meals. Midrats was usually a good meal, consisting of leftovers and anything easily made on the grill. Omelets, cheeseburgers, and one-eyed jacks (burger with egg on it), are favorites.

After some experimentation I started ordering a cheese omelet served on a cheeseburger (not just a burger—you have to have cheese on both). It eventually became known as the "Fat Joe." By the end of cruise, you could go up and ask for a Fat Joe and without hesitation be served a cheese omelet on a cheeseburger. Not terribly popular due to health issues; however, all who tried it were pleased!

Somehow, "Fat Joe" never caught on back home. However, a family favorite, "Mancakes" starts the day off right as well.

"Mancakes"

Serves 4–6

Ingredients:

Bacon (½–1 lb. as desired)
Potatoes (about 2 medium), diced
½ c. complete buttermilk pancake mix
⅓ c. Egg Beaters (or whole eggs if you prefer)
¼ c. milk

Sausage gravy mix, or homemade
Onions, breakfast sausage, peppers
  (optional)
Hot sauce (optional)

Directions:

Cut uncooked bacon slices across the grain, making small pieces about a half-inch long. Use as much as you want. Fry in pan (10-inch or so) until almost done. Do not drain.

Add potatoes and cook until potatoes are done and bacon is crisp to your own taste, about 10–15 minutes.

In a side bowl, mix: buttermilk pancake mix, Egg Beaters (whites or whole as you wish), and milk.

When bacon and potatoes are done, pour pancake mixture into pan. Move to medium heat—the idea is to cook the pancake without blackening the underside.

DO NOT FLIP until the bubbles do not fill in—it needs to cook well through. You will mess up the first few times trying to flip a 10-inch pancake. It's okay, keep trying.

While your Mancake is cooking, or before, prepare your Sausage Gravy mix (or make it from scratch).

After the Mancake is flipped, use the sausage gravy as if icing a cake. It will dry a bit on the hot Mancake, leaving a perfect topping.

Cut and serve as you would a pizza—in triangular slices.

Of course, substitutions and additions such as sausages, peppers, and onions are perfectly acceptable to personalize your own Mancake. The Cuba boys usually add a good dose of hot sauce as their signature move.

—Joseph A. Cuba
LCDR USN

The Greatest Generation

This cabin was built in 1929–1930 by Frank Enerson Sr., and his brother, Jacob, as a weekend retreat in the pinelands of New Jersey. Frank was a "Ship's Architect" in New York Harbor and the family lived in Staten Island.

The advent of the Depression found Frank unemployed and broke. The family moved to this cabin for the remainder of the Depression. Along with the cracked eggs story, great adventure stories of swinging in the pine trees and hard, wonderful times were often told by the three brothers, all veterans, Bob, Jack, Frank, and their baby sister Mary.

Due to the sacrifice and hard work of the "greatest generation," we live in peace and freedom, enjoying luxuries they could only dream of, such as Crab Benedict.

—*Christina Enerson*
Fairbanks, AK

THE ENERSON'S LAURELTON, N.J. 1930's FORT ST

Crab Benedict with Rosemary-Lemon Hollandaise

Serves 8

Ingredients:

Benedict set up:
4 English muffins, split and toasted
8 large eggs

Poaching liquid:
6 c. boiling water + 4 tbsp. white vinegar, mixed

Crab cake:
½ tsp. Old Bay seasoning
1 tbsp. sweet Thai chili sauce

½ tbsp. garlic, minced
1 large egg
1 tbsp. mayonnaise
1 tsp. yellow mustard
1 large red bell pepper, cleaned and diced
1 lb. crab meat (back fin meat preferred), drained
¾ c. Panko bread crumbs
½ tbsp. fresh parsley, chopped
3 tbsp. butter

Directions:

In large mixing bowl, whisk all crab cake ingredients together except the crab meat, Panko bread crumbs, butter, and parsley.

Add crab meat, tossing and mixing evenly. Add panko and parsley and toss again. Allow to rest in refrigerator for 10–15 mins.

Portion crab cakes into eight 2–3 oz. cakes

To cook crab cake:

Heat pan with butter. Add crab cakes to pan, browning both sides of the crab cake. Heat to internal temp of 150°F.

Poaching eggs:

Heat water to a medium boil.

Stir in one direction with sauce spoon then carefully drop the egg into the center of the whirlpool. The swirling water will help prevent the white from "feathering," or spreading out in the pan.

Allow to cook for 5 mins then remove egg from water with a perforated spoon.

Rosemary-Lemon Hollandaise:

Ingredients:

4 large egg yolks
1 to 2 tbsp. freshly squeezed lemon juice
½ c. unsalted butter, melted
½ tbsp. fresh rosemary leaves, finely chopped
Salt and pepper

Directions:

Vigorously whisk the egg yolks and 1 tablespoon lemon juice together in a stainless steel bowl until the mixture is thickened and doubled in volume.

Place the bowl over a saucepan containing barely simmering water (or use a double boiler). The water should not touch the bottom of the bowl. Continue to whisk rapidly. Be careful not to let the eggs get too hot or they will scramble.

Slowly drizzle in the melted butter and continue to whisk until the sauce is thickened and doubled in volume. Remove from heat, whisk in additional lemon juice to taste, rosemary, and a pinch of salt and pepper. Cover and place in a warm spot until ready to use for the eggs benedict.

If the sauce gets too thick, whisk in a few drops of warm water before serving.

Place your toasted half English muffin on a plate, and top with a crab cake. Add a poached egg to each crab cake, then drizzle your hollandaise sauce and garnish with your desired seasoning.

—David Enerson
Jacksonville, FL
Son of Barry Enerson, Cmdr, USN (Ret.), and grandson of WWII veteran Robert Enerson

Specialty pretzel buns by Randy Umfleet, Whipped Bakery, Lansing, MI.
Photo by Steve Dean Photography.

PART II: ASAP

Things That Can be Made in a Hurry

Pork Chop Tuesdays

The fun part of cooking, like most things in life, is the anticipation. Planning a small get together or special family meal with favorite ingredients, or just trying a new recipe is its own reward. But then there are what I call Pork Chop Tuesdays.

These are those everyday meals, when you arrive home tired from the day's work, and have to get something on the table. You pull some pork chops from the freezer and nuke in the microwave, perhaps warm up some leftovers, or order pizza and call it good.

A better option is to have a collection of fun, quick, and easy recipes, that can be prepared from pantry items and refrigerator or frozen staples. For example, if I am browning ground beef and/or Italian sausage, I will make a double or triple batch, and freeze the other two batches. They can be used later in dishes such as spaghetti sauce, chili, or shephard's pie. Before freezing, I label with the date and extra ingredients, such as onion, garlic, or mushrooms.

Presto! A home-cooked meal in less than thirty minutes.

—*Tracey Enerson Wood*
St. Petersburg, FL

Nachos

A great go-to meal for a busy weeknights. I always keep a bag of our favorite tortilla chips in the pantry.

Serving size: Depends on how many leftovers you need to use up!

Ingredients:

Favorite tortilla chips

Favorite cheese, grated (we use Tillamook Sharp Cheddar)

15-oz. can pinto or black beans, well drained

Sliced leftover chicken, beef, or pork

Chopped tomatoes

Chopped lettuce

Salsa

Directions:

Place the chips on an oven-safe plate.

Layer with your favorite grated cheese.

Add pinto or black beans.

Add whichever meat you have left over.

Heat to allow the cheese to melt—we place ours in the microwave for approximately 1 minute.

Now add chopped tomatoes and lettuce, and top with salsa.

—Carrie Woodard
Fairbanks, AK
Daughter of retired Army Vietnam vet and spouse of retired Army NCO

Wallisi Wall Banger

In early WWII, I was a Navy pilot stationed on Wallis Island in the South Pacific. We members of Scouting Squadron VS1D14 (later VS66) were charged with scaring Japanese submarines into constant submersions so they could not report the allies' island-hopping progress to their homeland.

Our squadron commander, Lt. J. L. Abbott Jr., conducted a mandatory "Happy Hour" each day for all officers. There was only one drink, which he labeled "Wallisi Wall Banger," after the island's name. It consisted of brandy and chocolate milk, the only ingredients available.

One afternoon I over-imbibed and decided that, after a year and a half of living in the jungle, and coping with heat, bugs, and dengue fever, it was time to go home. So I liberated a yellow inflatable life raft and started rowing for San Francisco.

When I reached the reef that surrounded our atoll, prudence replaced boredom, and I paddled back to camp, realizing that I had missed the evening's patrol I had been scheduled to fly (a fellow aviator had taken my place).

So, you have a "Wallisi Wall Banger" recipe: ½ brandy, ½ chocolate milk. As you might imagine, any substitution would be appropriate.

—Robert B. Reed
Cdr. US Navy (Ret.)

Pomegranate Cosmo

(Appropriate substitution for Wallisi Wall Banger)

Ingredients:
Agave (or honey, but agave is better)
Coarse sugar
1½ parts pomegranate juice (POM POM brand
    preferred)
1 part good vodka
¼ part Cointreau or Triple Sec
Fresh lime wedges

Directions:

Rim chilled martini glasses with a thin line of
agave or honey. Roll in sugar for a pretty rim.

Pour remaining ingredients, except for limes, into
an ice-filled shaker.

Shake it up for ten seconds, enough time to tell
one quick joke.

*Tip: Wearing your best Aloha shirt adds ambience.

Strain into prepared glasses.

Squeeze one lime wedge into each glass
and serve. Start next batch and keep 'em
coming.

—*Barry Enerson*
Cdr. US Navy (Ret.)
Stafford, VA

Barry with his wife, Janet Enerson, on St. Pete Beach,
FL. Drinking a Manhattan, because it's more manly.

A Kindness Remembered

When I was four months pregnant with our first child, my husband—a Navy Seabee—and I moved to Germany. Two months later he left for a handful of weeks. Our household shipment came during that time, so I decided to make a quick and easy casserole for myself to eat over the next few days while unpacking.

I preheated the oven, prepared the casserole, went to put it in to bake, and . . . nothing. The oven wasn't even the slightest bit warm. *Of course* it was broken. *Of course it was.* I had a miniature meltdown in the middle of our base apartment, feeling like I was drowning in a sea of boxes and homesickness. This was my first move as a military spouse and everything came crashing down on me in that moment.

But then I remembered that, between jetlag and continuous morning sickness, I had met the wife of my husband's coworker. She lived in the housing unit behind ours and

My great-grandfather, James S. Riley Sr., US Navy.

was the only number in my phone outside of my husband's. I hesitated—not one to ask for help or for comfortably making small talk—but I was so hungry and the casserole was ready to go.

The co-worker's wife didn't hesitate to let me bring the casserole over and use her oven. I didn't stay as it cooked, instead rushing home to scramble with the construction of our table so I had somewhere to eat it.

We never became more than acquaintances, and I haven't talked to her since she left Germany, but her helping me that day meant more than she could know.

Although they don't relate to this story, I'd also like to honor my grandfather and great-grandfather with these historical photos.

My grandfather, James S. Riley Jr., US Army.

Cheesy Chicken and Broccoli Casserole

Serves 4

Ingredients:

3 chicken breasts
16 oz. Velveeta cheese (more or less, depending on how cheesy you would like it)
1 (10-oz.) can cream of celery soup
10 oz. broccoli florets (fresh, or frozen and thawed)

Directions:

Cut the chicken and cheese into bite-sized pieces.

Mix the chicken, cheese, soup, and broccoli together. It may seem too dry before baking but once the cheese melts, it will be fine.

Transfer to a casserole dish and bake at 350°F for 30–45 minutes, or until chicken is cooked through.*

Serve over rice.

*Cooking times vary based on size and type of chicken pieces and size and shape of casserole dish. Ensure chicken is cooked through and no longer pink.

—Amber R. Duell
YA Author
Website: http://www.amberrduell.com/

Amber R. Duell with her husband and son.

The G-String

We had spent three years assigned to Fort Drum in upstate New York, home of the army's frequently deployed 10th Mountain Division. The people were warm, but the winters were rough.

One year, we had over two hundred inches of snow, and my husband had been deployed the entire winter. So I was less than enthused to be re-assigned there several years later, after all of our friends had gone, and my husband was about to take on one of the most challenging jobs of his career.

He was to be the G-3, in charge of operations for the division. He previously had served as an S-3, operations, at both battalion and brigade level. It is such a time-demanding position, I had begged him not to accept any more jobs that ended in 3. But there we were.

The moving van had departed, and I delved into what was by now routine, unpacking hundreds of boxes, and finding homes for our growing collection of essentials and bric-a-brac. Somehow, it is always easier to find the Christmas nutcrackers than the single towel you need right now.

June is a lovely time in upstate New York, so at about 4:00 p.m. I was taking a break on our front lawn when a minivan varoomed around a curve and screeched to a halt in front of our quarters.

The back door slid open. "Are you Tracey?" a pretty woman with light brown hair asked. Without waiting for an answer, she said, "Get in. We're going to welcome the new chief."

I did as I was told, after objecting that I had no gift prepared, as I was just moving in myself. The three other women in the van laughed, saying they had it covered. The van was brimming with cases of beer and bottles of wine, maybe a houseplant in there somewhere. They introduced themselves as Janet, Julia, and Melody (last names withheld to protect the guilty). They were the wives of the G-1, G-4, and G-2, all Lieutenant Colonels who worked under the division Chief of Staff. "Welcome to the G-string!" they shouted. I was still sliding the van door shut as we took off through the lush green woods that separated our housing area from that of the higher-ranking officers.

We arrived at the chief's home, which was in similar disarray to mine, with tall boxes stacked everywhere. The exception was that he had unpacked several dozen beer glasses, each

nearly three-feet high. He offered all of us a glass, and we proceeded to drink about two yards of beer each.

The chief was a hoot. He told story after story, about how he took his boat to work at the Pentagon to beat traffic, and many others that are for some reason blurry in my brain.

His cute blonde wife peeked out from a stack of boxes just once, took one look at us, and scurried away. We never saw her again. Literally. They split up soon after, and we always joked that the G-string scared her away.

We stayed on, laughing and telling stories for four hours. I was horrified to realize it was 8:00 p.m. We had overstayed at my husband's boss's home before he had even met him. Furthermore, my own family was probably starving for dinner and wondering where I was. (No cell phones back then.)

"Make something quick and delicious, they'll forgive you," Melody said, as we awaited a taxi ride home. "Like chicken and dumplings."

"Are you kidding, that takes hours!" I was thinking a trip to Anthony's Pizza was a more viable solution.

"Not the way I make it." Melody told me how she makes the dish, quick and delicious. I've since tweaked it a bit, and it remains a family favorite, twenty years later.

Our second tour of Fort Drum turned out to be lots of fun.

☆☆☆☆☆☆☆☆☆☆☆☆

Quick Chicken and Dumplings

About 35 minutes to prepare; serves 4

Ingredients:

2 tbsp. butter
1 small onion, chopped
2 stalks celery, chopped
1 qt. low-salt chicken broth
8 oz. water
1 tsp. celery seed
2 bay leaves
Freshly ground black pepper

1½–2 lb. boneless, skinless chicken breasts
    or thighs
½ c. baby carrots, chopped (optional)
1 can unbaked biscuit dough (5 large
    biscuits), home-style or buttermilk flavor
Fresh parsley or baby spinach (optional)

Directions:

Sauté onion and celery in butter in a 4–5 quart pot. You can skip this step if in a real hurry, and just add vegetables to the broth.

Add broth, water, celery seed, bay leaves, and black pepper. Simmer a few minutes, or longer if desired.

Add chicken, and carrots, if using them, and simmer until chicken is no longer pink in the center, about 10–15 minutes.

Remove chicken and vegetables from the broth and keep warm. Shred or chop chicken into bite-size pieces.

Add salt and pepper to taste. There is also salt in the broth, so don't overdo it.

Cut each raw biscuit into four wedges. Place wedges in simmering broth, half of them at a time. Cook, turning several times, until center is fluffy, not gooey, about 5 minutes.

Repeat with other half of dough wedges. This gives you 20 dumplings.

Remove bay leaves. Add hot broth to chicken and vegetables, top with dumplings, and serve.

Garnish with fresh parsley or baby spinach if desired.

—Tracey Enerson Wood
St. Petersburg, FL
Author of A Bridge Between Us

How Wig Wags
Led to Naughty Island Drinks

The current mission statement of the United States Army Signal Corps (USASC) contains such advanced terms as "multi-channel satellite," "terrestrial microwave," and "video-teleconferencing." The corps provides "a seamless . . . network . . ." to support Army, joint, and coalition military operations.

All this started with two wig-wag flags. The US Army Signal Corps was born in 1860 at the urging of army medical officer Albert James Myer, who advocated the use of flags (torches at night) to signal between soldiers in combat.

Its early use of tethered aerial observation balloons during the Battle of Bull Run led to the development of the national weather service, NOAA, and the Army Air Corps, the forerunner of the US Air Force. The development of the country's wired telegraph and telephone lines was initially the exclusive province of the USASC.

The Corps shepherded the world into the modern global information age. Technological advances in communication exploded during both world wars. During World War II, forward outposts came to rely on small portable generator units to meet their power needs. Many manufacturing companies such as Onan and Briggs & Stratton made thousands of these for the military. The Wisconsin Company became a successful supplier when, in 1944, it developed a 4-cycle 1800 RPM internal combustion engine paired with a 2.5 kilowatt generator. This compact unit was light enough to be transported by one or two men in combat conditions.

After the war, many unused USASC generators wound up for sale from army surplus stocks. Sam Parlin, a druggist and consummate tinkerer from Old Town, Maine, had served in the Army Air Service during and after WWI. In 1938 he and a partner built a log cabin on lakeside land in eastern Maine, and named it Timberock.

This remote location was then only reachable by logging trails made and used by teams of work horses. The closest road used by motorized traffic was a gravel highway a mile away. Much backbreaking work slowly improved the logging trail to be barely usable by a carefully driven car or truck.

Sam sold his share of Timberock to his partner and built his own cabin in 1949. As a little boy, I remember watching Sam, his wife, Amy, and a crew of men lay the logs for the second cabin, which they christened Timberock II.

Before long, in this land of ice boxes, kerosene lamps, wood stoves, and two-holers, Sam installed an unheard of modern convenience in Timberock II: electricity! There weren't even electric poles on the Airline, the winding, dusty, 100-mile main route to the Maritime Provinces of Canada.

The source of this ultra-modern convenience was a United States Army Signal Corps PE108-E AC/DC Wisconsin generator Sam had purchased from army surplus.

For years he used it to provide a few electric lights, and a receptacle for a television with a snowy screen. Often Sam and Amy could be seen watching Lawrence Welk on their vertical hold challenged TV, on evenings when WABI out of Bangor was transmitting more than just a test pattern.

Sam even installed a remote starter box in the cabin, wired to a 12-volt automobile battery. All this was stock green US Army surplus equipment that came with the unit. Ah, the luxury of it all! Sam and Amy had no children, and when they sold Timberock II to my wife and me in 1980, we inherited all its contents and appurtenances, including pots, pans, mismatched chinaware, photos, guest books, wood stoves, squirrels, mice, and all fixtures, including the generator.

We immediately returned our newly acquired cabin to a more primitive place by removing the blasphemous lights and wiring. However, I moved the generator from its own little lean-to shelter outside the back door onto the seat bench of an unused privy inside the attached woodshed. I ran the wiring harness to the control box in the kitchen beside the propane refrigerator and the large, red-handled pump at the sink across from the cook stove. I piped the exhaust out through the shed wall and into a five-gallon bucket of water for an effective muffler which still sounds like that of an inboard motor boat.

The A/C outlet on the control box is exclusively dedicated for blender use and the blender is used only to make frozen rum-based drinks which are served at sundown on the deck overlooking the lake. My niece, Katie, recognizing a taste reminiscent of the Caribbean and respecting the strength of the libation, inadvertently named these drinks by asking one afternoon, "Uncle Doug, are you making any of those 'naughty island drinks' this evening?" The name stuck and now the entire neighborhood knows where to go to have a "naughty island drink" at sundown.

Naughty Island Drink

My recipe for this frozen concoction is no secret!

Serves 4

Ingredients:

8 oz. frozen lemonade concentrate
6 oz. white rum
2 oz. coconut flavored rum
1 ripe banana
Ice

Directions:

Dump the contents of an 8-oz. can of frozen lemonade concentrate into the blender.

Fill the empty can with ¾ white rum and ¼ coconut flavored rum (or adjust to desired strength). Pour the rum into the blender and toss in a peeled banana (the riper, the better).

Fill the blender up with ice.

Doug Clapp and his niece enjoy generator-fueled libations.

Push the starter switch on the remote box until you hear the familiar bubbling of the generator muffler (optional for those flatlanders on the grid).

Puree until the contents stop rumbling and thrashing and the sudden change of pitch of the machine indicates that the ice has reached the consistency of slush.

Serve in sturdy, plastic, drop-proof goblets.

WARNING: These drinks are strong! The first drink tastes like a second one. Thereafter, operation of machinery or telling complicated stories including multi-syllabic words is discouraged.

—Douglas Clapp
St. Petersburg, FL

From Army Brat to Army Spouse

I met Jim, my husband of thirty-nine years, in 1977, while he was stationed at Fort Benning, Georgia. My own father had been in the Army and had retired after twenty-three years of service outside of Fort Benning, in Columbus, Georgia. My father had served in World War II while in the Marines; he then joined the Army after completing college. My father had three more combat tours, once in Korea and twice in Vietnam.

Jim's family was also an Army family of thirty years. His father is a World War II veteran who found himself on the European front. His mother was the consummate hostess and loved to have family and friends over. My own mother did not love entertaining, so I learned most tricks

My mother and father, Col. (Ret.) Willis B. (Andy) Anderson, and Ruth Anderson Safar, 1952.

of the trade from my mother-in-law. I have four stories to share: one from my own childhood, one from my early years as a wife, and then two from my time as a Senior Spouse.

Growing up, I was a picky eater and loved cookies and sweets. We lived on a modest income and did not run to fast food restaurants often. Actually, the only one we had when I was a child was McDonalds, and even those were rare! So my mother taught me the easiest cookie recipe that there ever could be, and uses ingredients that most homes would find in their cupboards. After my mother's passing at the age of eighty-nine, I found a hand-written copy of this recipe and had it reproduced and now have it framed in my kitchen.

No-Bake Chocolate Oatmeal Cookies

Makes about 9 large cookies

Ingredients:

2 c. sugar

½ c. whole milk

½ c. cocoa powder

¼ c. butter

2 c. rolled oats (I use quick-cooking but have also used regular oats)

½ c. peanut butter (I have used smooth and crunchy)

½ c. nuts, optional

1 tsp. vanilla

Photo by Steve Dean Photography

Directions:

Mix first four ingredients well in a small pan over medium heat. Bring to a boil and cook for 2 minutes.

Add remaining ingredients.

Stir and drop by spoonfuls on waxed paper. Let cool and set.

Store in air-tight container—these will also freeze well.

From my mother, Ruth Anderson Safar.

Author's note: Also tested with light butter and low-fat milk. Tasted great, but the cookies were rather sticky. Much better texture using regular butter.

—Carol Campbell
Wife of LTG (Ret.) Jim Campbell

Soldier-Seaman Bryce

Following graduation from high school in Buffalo, New York, my father, Milt Bryce, and many of his classmates joined the Army. After boot camp he was put on leave and returned home to Buffalo. His mother was a bit embarrassed that her son was home so long doing nothing except wearing his uniform around town.

After a while, my father became restless and went with another group of high school friends and joined the Navy. Again, he went through boot camp and was put on a ship out on the Atlantic. One day, the Shore Patrol picked him up off of his ship and returned him to land, where he was turned over to Army Military Police. He was taken to an Army post where he was brought up before the commanding officer, who demanded to know where my father had been.

Dad explained he had been put on leave by the Army for a long time and, thinking they had forgotten about him, he joined the Navy. The C.O. was flummoxed; he couldn't bring my father up on charges as he really hadn't deserted. He then asked my father what branch of the service he wanted to stay in, Army or Navy? Being a young man, my father wasn't sure what he should do, so he asked the C.O. for his advice.

The officer told him he could either stay in the Navy and be returned to his ship, or return to the Army where he would be put on leave until they could reassign him. He chose the latter and was sent back to Buffalo. As he left the office, the C.O. said to my father, "And kid, don't let me hear that you joined the Marines or the Coast Guard."

This explains why my father had two sets of uniforms; he was a rare individual who had served in two branches of the military at the same time.

Following this, PFC Bryce was assigned to the Army Air Corps and trained in Laredo, Texas, becoming a flight engineer on B-17s and B-24s.

This recipe is based on the food served in his training camp at Laredo, Texas.

Slop

Simple to make and feeds at least four people.

Ingredients:
1 lb. ground beef
1 (14–15-oz.) can spaghetti
1 (15-oz.) can pork & beans
1 small onion, chopped
½ green bell pepper, chopped
Salt & pepper to taste
Garlic powder to taste

Directions:

1. Brown meat in skillet and discard the fat.

2. Add the other ingredients and heat through. Serve.

—Tim Bryce
Tampa Bay, FL
Syndicated columnist and radio commentator. His blog is at timbryce.com

Vegetables Incognito

My father-in-law and mother-in-law, COL (Ret.) John (Jack) and Mary Campbell, at his retirement, Fort McClellan, AL, 1968.

Shortly after I had married, we were home in Alabama, visiting my husband's family. His mother was hosting a rather large gathering of friends, as we were home and everyone needed to see us! I was a picky eater as a child, and my husband did not eat a large variety of vegetables at that time.

His mother had prepared a casserole and he was on his way back for his third helping. His mother had noticed and was so excited, she said, "I am so happy you like my squash casserole."

My husband's face fell and he could not make himself eat anymore.

Squash Casserole

Serves 8

Ingredients:
1 stick of butter or margarine
1 (14–16-oz.) pkg. herb dressing (stuffing mix)
2 c. cooked summer squash, sliced and well drained
1 medium onion, grated or finely chopped
2 medium carrots, grated or shredded
1 (10–11-oz.) can condensed cream of mushroom soup
½ pint sour cream
Salt and pepper to taste

Directions:

Melt butter or margarine and mix with herb dressing.

In another bowl, mix all other ingredients.

Spread half of the dressing mix over bottom of 9x13 pan.

Add all of squash mixture on top then cover with remaining dressing mix.

Bake at 350°F oven for 30 minutes.

Recipe of Mary Campbell
Submitted by Carol Campbell
Wife of LTG (Ret.) Jim Campbell

Bacon Balls

My father liked to be called "Daddio" for reasons never given, probably because he liked to be different. For one thing, he loved bacon. He cooked it every Sunday, a whole pound of it. But he wouldn't lay it out in neat strips like most people. He would scramble it up on high heat with enthusiasm, until there was nothing left but crisp bacon balls.

Daddio served in the Army during WWII, but rarely spoke of it. Once in a while he would drink apple brandy, and mention a French farm family who gave him Calvados. If really pressed for a story, he would tell us about the pigs.

During the Battle of the Bulge, Dad was in Belgium, and had been fighting in the front lines for about six months. The troops were fatigued from fighting, worn from the constant movement toward Germany, and frequently hungry, due to difficulties with supplies. The hunger is something he would never mention directly. Rather, he'd talk about the kindness of the people, how they would give the soldiers half of their family's loaf of bread, or 'accidentally' leave a bucket of potatoes in a field for them.

In rare moments, he would tell us of the family in Belgium who risked their lives hiding him in the cellar of their barn after he got trapped behind enemy lines. He remained in touch with this family for decades, but sadly, none of the letters still exist.

The winter of 1944–45 was bitterly cold. In the surviving pictures, I recognize his brilliant smile, matching the snowy landscape surrounding him. He didn't smile when talking about the pigs. His unit had been moving rapidly across the countryside, in between battles with the Germans. At night, they would find an existing hole, perhaps a shallow well or animal shelter, or dig a foxhole to sleep in.

One morning he woke up in a trench, with the usual hunger pangs, filthy and shivering. He wiggled his toes to make sure they were still there. Hearing grunts and squeals, he looked up to see a family of pigs staring down at him. The biggest pig kneeled down and sniffed him, his nose dripping onto Daddio's face.

That, he said, was his lowest moment, even lower than hiding in the basement of a barn. There could be nothing lower than lying in a ditch, beneath a common pig. After that, the rest of the war, the rest of his life, could only be better.

And that was always his attitude. No matter what trials life brought him (and there were many) nothing would be lower than having pig slime dripped on him from above. And maybe, just maybe, this explains the bacon balls.

God bless you, Daddio.

—Tracey Enerson Wood
St. Petersburg, FL

Robert Enerson Sr., Belgium, Winter 1944–1945.

Bacon Wrapped Dates

Note: Super easy to prepare, can be put together the day before an event, then cooked on demand. They will disappear, guaranteed!

Makes about 12 appetizer servings

Ingredients:
1 lb. regular sliced bacon
1 lb. pitted dates

Directions:

With bacon slices unseparated, cut across the slab, so each slice is halved in length.

Wrap a half slice of bacon around each date, and secure with toothpick.

Bake on low broil until bacon is crisp, about 10–15 minutes.

—Kristen Riffle
Oslo, Norway
Granddaughter of Robert Enerson Sr.

Ingredients for a Happy Marriage

First off, let me just say, being a military spouse came with its fair share of surprises. I suppose every marriage does, but there were definitely some major ones due to marrying someone in the army.

I was in my late twenties when I finally decided to take the plunge, and drop everything I had—a lifestyle most people dream of! Happy hours constantly, sushi, Indian, Mexican, Columbian, Thai, Korean, or Greek food whenever, or celebrating meatless Mondays, all at least once a week either for lunch or dinner! I didn't know what real barbeque tasted like; I'd never ordered any fried food dish in my entire life, much less cooked it! I can honestly tell you I had never had fried chicken or catfish until I started dating my stereotypical all-American, macho, and extremely handsome husband.

So began my first major challenge marrying my husband: What to cook for him? I want to make him happy, but I am super stubborn and looooved the kind of food I had been eating the past ten years of my life, which was diverse in spices, veggies, legumes, and light on meat!

The difficulties commenced when I made a Greek- inspired meal which I believed was absolutely delicious, and was surprised when my husband barely ate it, "politely" commenting there wasn't enough meat in it! Then I made an Italian-inspired dish but substituted spaghetti noodles with zucchini noodles. Surprisingly, once again he barely ate it, "politely" mentioning how nothing can substitute the "great taste of pasta!"

Well, one of the only meals he never "politely" commented on was a simple stir fry! It's quick, easy, and you can go *super* heavy on vegetables and/or meat and make everyone happy! Plus, you can always add in a side of jasmine rice, and everyone knows a meal with jasmine rice can never go wrong! Your kids get all the veggies they need, and your husband gets all the red, heavy, beefiness he craves—win-win!

And now there are five of us!
Photo by Firehorse Entertainment

Beef and Vegetable Stir Fry

Ingredients:

1½ lb. skirt steak, sliced thinly against the grain
⅓ c. + 3 tbsp. soy sauce
1 tbsp. oyster sauce
4 tsp. cornstarch
1 tsp. black pepper
2 tbsp. water
2 tbsp. vegetable oil
2 bell peppers, sliced into thin strips
1 large onion, sliced into thin strips
½ lb. fresh broccoli florets
1 c. snap peas

Directions:

Place thinly sliced skirt steak in a bowl and add 3 tablespoons soy sauce, 1 tablespoon oyster sauce, 2 teaspoons cornstarch, and black pepper.

In a small bowl, mix ⅓ cup soy sauce, water, and 2 teaspoons cornstarch. Set aside.

Heat a wok or large pan on medium-high heat. Swirl in 1 tablespoon of the oil and add the beef, spreading evenly in the wok. Cook undisturbed for 20 seconds, letting the beef brown.

Using a spatula, stir meat, cooking another 3–4 minutes. Transfer to a plate.

Add remaining tablespoon of oil to wok, along with peppers and onions, and cook about 2 minutes. Add broccoli and cook another 2 minutes. Add snap peas and return beef to the wok.

Add the sauce and stir fry about 1 minute until slightly thickened.

—Allison Wood
Bettendorf, IA

PART III: FIT FOR DUTY
Healthy Choices

Induction Physical

In 1967, most United States medical interns were drafted into the Vietnam War. Although my active duty status was deferred until the end of my surgical training, I was a lieutenant in the inactive naval reserve. Part of my orders read, "You are to report to Jacksonville Naval Air Station at 1100 November 10th for your induction physical examinations."

Although Jacksonville was two hundred miles from Tampa, we would pass by Daytona Beach on the way. My goal was to spend several hours on the beach on my way home from the naval base. Arriving at 10:30 a.m. with orders in hand, I entered the large one-story gray medical complex. A sizeable waiting area filled with many young men and a few young women were awaiting their enlistment physical. A queue was formed just inside the door, where orders were reviewed and a history form issued. The enlistees then sat down until a corpsman appeared to direct the history-taking process. He would ask questions for the form, "Have you ever had _____, _____?" until the form was completed.

This could be a long day, I thought, and called a corpsman over. "I'm Dr. Endicott, here for an induction physical. I could expedite the history process by filling out my own form."

"Yes sir, Lieutenant. I will just call over Chief Corpsman Light to facilitate your processing."

Chief Light, a slim, bespeckled corpsman, with many hash marks on his chest insignia, stepped from behind the front registration desk and walked over to me. "If you have completed your history form, follow me to the next station for the hearing test."

After the audiogram was performed in the small audio booth, we went to the adjacent hematology room where a vein in the left antecubital area was secured by a needle in the first attempt.

As we moved through these stations, I was introduced by Chief Light to his fellow corpsman as a VIP, causing mild excitement among the medical staff. In the radiology room, I was told, "stand in front of the wall-mounted X-ray film with your chin up and your hands over your head" for the chest X-ray.

"Don't you think I should remove my pen and paper from my pocket?"

"Yes sir! Sorry, sir!"

Across the hall from the radiology department was a door marked Medical Staff Officer. Chief Light knocked, stuck his head in the doorway and said, "There is someone out here to see you, Dr. Levine."

A loud voice came from the room. "Is it the women?"

"No sir. Lieutenant Endicott is here for his physical."

"Send him in."

Dr. Levine was a short, slightly overweight man, wearing white long pants, shoes, socks, and short sleeved shirt with two gold stripes on each shoulder. He stood up for our hand shake and, after we sat down we began to visit socially. He was from Miami originally and came to this base after his internship by way of the draft.

He soon asked, "You don't want a physical exam, do you?"

Surprised, I said, "That's the reason I'm here!"

"This is my last day in the military," he said. "You look healthy. I would say blood pressure 120/70 and pulse 72 and regular." He continued to dry lab my physical until he closed the chart to end our meeting.

"What are you going to do when you get out?" I asked.

"I've seen so many healthy patients over the past two years, that I have a pathology residency waiting for me at Dade County General."

Epilogue

That afternoon on Daytona Beach, I speculated about my future in the Navy.

—*James N. Endicott, MD.*
Captain (Ret.), US Navy Reserves

Korean Cuisine Trifecta

There are around thirty thousand US military service members stationed in the Republic of Korea (ROK, or South Korea), so it's not unusual to come across military members and veterans who have spent some time on "the peninsula." A common theme you will hear is how delicious and interesting Korean food can be.

I was fortunate enough to be stationed in South Korea twice, once in the sprawling mega-metropolis of Seoul, and later in the small Navy town of Chinhae, not far from the coastal city of Busan. During those two tours, I never ran out of interesting things to eat, ranging from standard Korean street barbeque to exotic seafood dishes, and everything in between.

In my mind, Korean cuisine is best associated with a simple trifecta: delicious meat, fresh vegetables, and simple rice. It is often served in a communal fashion with unique and interesting side dishes that are often spicy and full of garlic, in addition to dozens of variations on fermented vegetables called Kimchi. Honestly, what's not to like?

A typical meal at a Korean restaurant will usually focus on some form of grill or hot plate in the center of the table, upon which guests are able to cook the fresh ingredients themselves so that the food can be consumed almost immediately. Many restaurants use natural gas burners, but you can find some that will keep a large fire running to maintain glowing red-hot charcoals that they will bring to the table using welders' gloves and heavy vice-grips.

Side dishes are always shared, sometimes accompanied by "friendship shots" of Soju, the Korean national spirit. Once the raw main ingredients are delivered to the table, guests can start cooking on the communal grill, giving everyone a chance to participate in the cooking process, which builds a sense of comradery and shared ownership in the outcome of the meal.

There are plenty of other aspects and features of Korean cuisine, enough to fill numerous cookbooks on their own merits. But if one had to pick a single dish that perfectly encapsulates Korean cuisine, I think many would agree it is Bibimbap. Simply a translation for "mixed rice," Bibimbap is the ultimate comfort dish consisting of rice, some form of cut or shredded meat, fresh vegetables, an egg, and sauce derived from a uniquely Korean spicy chili and garlic paste called Gochujang.

The recipes for Bibimbap can vary a bit, probably because there is no fixed definition for the ingredients; preparation is open to interpretation by the cook. (Sometime it's just a good

excuse to clean out the fridge.) Regardless of how it's prepared, Bibimbap is always a solid go-to dish when you have a hankering for Korean food.

When possible, another important variation is the Dolsot version of Bibimbap, which is served in a thick stone bowl that has been pre-heated to scalding temperatures to help cook the ingredients and maintain their heat. With Dolsot Bibimbap, the egg can also be served raw on top of the vegetable heap, since the heat from the stone bowl and ingredients should ensure the egg is cooked thoroughly once mixed. Another treat comes at the end of the dish, when the rice near the bottom of the stone bowl has attained a nice crunchy texture due to the extreme heat.

So if you'd like to try out some Korean food, I'd strongly recommend finding a good Korean restaurant that serves Dolsot Bibimbap, and then give it a shot at home. Aside from finding the Gochujang paste, the ingredients are incredibly simple, and the dish is always a fulfilling crowd pleaser that gives you a little taste of the wonderful delight that is Korean cuisine.

Note: If using stone bowls for Dolsot Bibimbap, preheat the bowls in the oven or on a stove top until they are extremely hot, and drizzle some sesame oil on the bowl before adding the rice. If you go this route, be extremely careful when handling the stone bowls, and be sure to have a non–heat conducting dish, such as wood, to place the bowl on top of when serving.

☆☆☆☆☆☆☆☆☆☆☆☆☆☆☆

Bibimbap

Makes two bowls

Ingredients:

1 lb. beef (can use shredded or ground beef, or cuts like a round, ribeye, or sirloin)

Meat Marinade:

3 tbsp. soy sauce
2 tbsp. sesame oil
1 tbsp. vinegar or rice wine
1 tbsp. roasted sesame seeds
1 tbsp. honey or brown sugar
2–3 garlic cloves, minced

2 c. medium grain white rice
2 eggs
1 large carrot
1 large zucchini

1 large bunch spinach
2 c. bean sprouts
2 c. mushrooms
6 garlic cloves, minced
1 scallion
Sesame oil and seeds
Salt and pepper

Sauce:

3 tbsp. gochujang paste
2 tbsp. sesame oil
1 tbsp. vinegar or rice wine
1 tbsp. roasted sesame seeds
1 tbsp. honey or brown sugar
2–3 garlic cloves, minced

Directions:

Meat Preparation:

Mix all marinade ingredients together. Whatever cut of beef you use, you should marinate the meat beforehand for a few hours with the same ingredients that you will use for the sauce, but with soy sauce replacing the gochujang paste.

If using any type of steak cut, cut the steak into thin strips.

Do NOT re-use the marinade to make the gochujang sauce as it will have raw meat juices mixed into it. After marinating, put some oil in a pan on medium heat and cook your beef thoroughly and then set aside.

Rice:

Cook rice according to package directions, and while waiting you can prepare the rest of the ingredients. Be sure to keep rice warm prior to transferring into the bowls.

continued on page 62

Vegetables:

For proper presentation of the Bibimbap, the individual vegetables are portioned around the bowl in sections, therefore you will need to prepare them all separately before combining them.

Note also that you do not have to stick to this list of vegetables. These are just suggestions of what is commonly used.

Bean Sprouts:

Bring some salted water to a light boil. Add bean sprouts and cook for 2–3 minutes to blanch. Remove and rinse with cold water in a colander.

Drizzle with sesame oil, then add 2 cloves of minced garlic, a pinch of sesame seeds, and a pinch of salt and pepper. Mix and set aside.

Spinach:

Blanch similarly to the bean sprouts—bring some salted water to a light boil. Add spinach and cook for no more than 1 minute. Remove and rinse with cold water in a colander.

Take a knife and cut the spinach a couple times to ensure it isn't too long and stringy. Drizzle with sesame oil, then add 2 cloves of minced garlic, a pinch of sesame seeds, and a pinch of salt and pepper. Mix and place to the side.

Zucchini:

You can either julienne zucchini, or slice it into semi circles. Drizzle with sesame oil, then add 1 diced scallion, 2 cloves of minced garlic, a pinch of sesame seeds, and a pinch of salt and pepper. Cook on medium heat with oil for 2–3 minutes, then remove and set aside.

Carrots:

Julienne your carrot into matchstick-sized pieces. Cook them in a pan on medium heat with some oil and salt to flavor. Just cook them for a few minutes, then place to the side.

Mushrooms:

Chop mushrooms. Cook in a pan on medium heat for a few minutes with some oil and salt to flavor. Drain off any excess liquid, then place to the side.

Gochujang Sauce:

The most important part of the Bibimbap is the sauce. It's derived mostly from Korean Gochujang paste, which is made from red chili and soy beans with salty and sweet flavoring added, and is typically fermented similar to Korean Kimchi.

The sauce for the Bibimbap is simply Gochujang paste with a few things added to make it a little more sauce-like and flavorful. Simply mix the sauce ingredients above together in a bowl.

Add additional water as needed to thin the sauce if it is still too thick. Add more honey or brown sugar if you like it a little sweeter.

The Gochujang paste will be pretty salty to begin with so don't use soy sauce to thin, and definitely don't add any additional salt.

(Note: If you are desperate and can't find a local Korean food store to buy real Gochujang or similar Ssamjang then I suppose you can substitute Sriracha sauce, but I strongly recommend trying to find the Gochujang first. It's absolutely delicious and I would probably eat it with everything if it were socially acceptable.)

Eggs:

Fry eggs in an oiled skillet sunny-side up—do not overcook, you want the yolk as runny as possible.

Final preparation:

Once your eggs are finished, place a thick layer of rice in the bottom of two bowls.

Layer your meat and each of your prepared vegetables on top of the rice, placing a small portion of each ingredient in a clockwise pattern around the bowl.

You will want the ingredients hot, so reheat your rice and vegetables in the microwave or in an oven as needed. Once the rice and vegetables are sufficiently hot, place the fried egg on top, then drizzle with sesame oil and seeds.

Then drizzle your Gochujang sauce on top, depending on how spicy you want it.

Tip: *When eating the Bibimbap, use your chop sticks to break open the egg yolk and mix the various ingredients together. Also, it is perfectly acceptable to also use a spoon to help scoop up the ingredients when you reach the bottom of the bowl, as using chop sticks to pick up the last little bits can be tricky.*

—*Scott Riffle*
US Navy

In the Elbow of Big Sur

Artichokes and crawdads, though an unlikely pair, were the peanut butter and jelly pillars in my family's food foundation. When I was four, we moved to what I like to call the Elbow of Big Sur. Right where Route 1 bends sharply to the left, less than thirty minutes from Castroville (the artichoke capital of the world), in the shadow of the Point Sur lighthouse was the Point Sur Naval Facility (NAVFAC), an unnoticeable blip in the magnificence of the Scenic Route 1 coastline. This tiny little neighborhood was where I learned to ride a bike, met my lifelong best friend, and where we would build my greatest childhood memories.

Almost every Saturday in the summers we would spend the afternoon streaming (not watching videos on our nonexistent iPhones) for crawdads and eating artichokes. Dad would run to fisherman's wharf first thing to grab a few fish carcasses while my mom would prepare a picnic. In the afternoon, when the coastal fog lifted, we would drive about ten minutes down the road to Big Sur River.

We often went with family friends. Most frequently with my lifelong best friend's family. Let's call her Radio (my dad called her that because she was always singing when the radio was on). She and I met playing on the base and went to kindergarten together. Our fathers both attended the Naval Postgraduate School. Our families became great friends, visiting each other every few years wherever we were stationed. When Radio and I ran into each other (she was supposed to be in Alaska!) at freshman year orientation at Virginia Tech, we instantly picked up where we left off. She ended up staying in Virginia and now our kids are growing up together.

James Thomas, LTC (Ret) US Army.

Now back to the crawdaddies! A stone-tied fish carcass would be thrown in after we picked one of our usual spots along the river. After a cold one, my dad would suit up with his snorkeling mask and gloves. The water at its warmest was maybe 50 degrees. He

almost never wore a wet suit, although he did get hypothermia once. He described the underwater scene as "something that could only be seen in a sci-fi movie with crayfish covering the fish in a feeding frenzy. They were in such a frenzy, that in one breath I could pluck them off one by one and put them between each of my fingers on my left hand. I could get five or six on one breath, come up, and do my NBA slam dunk into my five gallon bucket until it was three quarters full."

Our biggest haul was when the two families filled an inflatable boat full of crawdads and we proceeded to walk them upstream. It was a proud moment.

Back at home we'd prepare the feast. Along with the crawdads were grilled artichokes and garlic bread. I remember the artichokes being almost as big as my head. I still smile when I think of how satisfying it was to scrape a morsel of artichoke flesh off the petal with my bottom front teeth.

Having previously moved from the DC area, we prepared our crawdads like a Maryland blue crab. We would set a huge strainer over a beer bath and steam the crawdads, dump them ritualistically over newspaper-wrapped tables, and sprinkle them with Old Bay.

There's nothing like sharing a table with great friends, foraged food, and traditions I will never forget. I'm fortunate the short staccato living of military life has afforded me somewhat of a full circle. My parents were stationed back near the Big

The Thomas and Wood families enjoy Big Sur, circa 1987.

Sur River and decided to retire there. We visit them every summer. One day, Radio and I will both make it back to take our kids fishing for crawdads although I doubt either of our husbands can "hang with the big boys" (as my dad says) and brave the water with no wetsuit.

Big Boy Artichokes

Serves 4

Ingredients:
4 large artichokes
Salt
1 rib celery
1 lemon
1 tbsp. olive oil

Balsamic vinaigrette:
2 garlic cloves, minced
2 tbsp. minced Italian parsley
½ c. balsamic vinegar
¼ c. good extra-virgin olive oil
Salt and pepper to taste
Dash of Tabasco

Apricot aioli: (Mom's dipping choice)
1 tbsp. apricot jam or jelly
½ c. mayonnaise

Directions:

Bring a large pot of salted water to a rolling boil. The water should be salty like the ocean the artichokes didn't come from.

Add the celery rib.

Prepare the artichokes by peeling off any brown or bad parts. Peel a layer off of the stems with a vegetable peeler, trim the brown ends of the stem, and if you'd like to be extra gentle to your dinner guests, trim off the thorn at the tip of each petal with scissors.

Cut the artichokes in half and immediately place them in a bowl of cold water with a lemon, cut in half and squeezed. They will oxidize slightly as you prep the remaining ingredients.

When all the artichokes have been prepped, remove them from their lemon water and boil for 30–40 minutes.

Prepare the balsamic vinaigrette and apricot aioli by mixing all the ingredients for each.

After 30 minutes, check the artichokes for doneness by pulling a petal off the artichoke. If it removes easily, they're ready.

Drain and allow the artichokes to cool cut side up on a sheet tray. Once the artichokes are cool enough to handle, scoop out the hairy choke using a small spoon. Keep scooping until you don't see any hair.

Preheat a grill to medium high and grill both sides for 5 minutes, cut side down first.

Spoon the balsamic over the artichokes once you flip them face up and grill their bottoms. Serve hot with additional vinaigrette spooned in the center or apricot aioli.

In case you don't know how to eat an artichoke, don't worry. Peel a petal off. Dip it in your sauce of choice. Turn the petal upside down so the curve faces towards you and the leafy part is at the top. Bite down gently and using your bottom teeth, scrape the flesh from the petal. Repeat. When the heart of the artichoke is exposed, and there are no more petals attached, eat your heart out!

—*Olivia Devescovi*
Herndon, VA
Daughter of Sunny and
James Thomas, LTC, US Army (Ret.)

An Evening Emulated

While assigned to the Rock of the Marne Division (3rd Infantry Division), my wife and I were guests at the home of the 1st Brigade Commander and his lovely wife. As they had recently returned from a vacation in Alaska where they had caught numerous wild halibut, we were treated to delicious grilled halibut steaks.

Possessing the culinary skills of a halibut, I had the good fortune to observe my host as he grilled the halibut steaks, and fifteen years later, I had the good fortune to try the technique myself using Atlantic salmon filets.

Now I am able to not only grill salmon filets, but also produce consistent results on a repetitive basis.

Dave and Sue Washechek in 2001.

Grilled Atlantic Salmon (Marne Sapper Style)

Here is the magic.

Serves 4

Ingredients:

1 side fresh Atlantic* salmon, de-boned but skin on
6 tbsp. olive oil

3 tbsp. Old Bay seasoning
3 tbsp. lemon pepper
3 tsp. ground black pepper

Of course, you can substitute King, Red, or Silver salmon, if you are lucky enough to get some.

Directions:

Pour half the olive oil in a rectangular baking pan large enough to hold the salmon filet. Place the filet skin-side down on the olive oil in the baking pan.

Pour remaining olive oil over the flesh-side of the filet and cover uniformly with the Old Bay Seasoning, lemon pepper, and ground black pepper.

Warm grill to 350°F. Once the grill is heated to temperature, lay the salmon skin-side down directly onto the grilling surface. I suggest using two wide spatulas when handling the filet. Discard the marinade the fish was sitting in.

Grill until the lower half of the filet nearest the heat turns from pink to white, approximately 4–5 minutes, depending on the thickness of the fish. Using two wide spatulas, slice between the skin and flesh through the layer of fat and flip the filet, placing it on the skin that will be stuck to the grill surface.

Grill until the "new" lower half of the filet nearest the heat turns from pink to white, approximately 4–5 minutes, depending on the thickness of the fish.

Using two wide spatulas, transfer the filet to a flat plate or board and allow the fish to rest for 10 minutes. Remove the skin and serve warm.

—David Washechek
Col. (Ret.) US Army
Katy, TX

London 2012: The Carrot Invasion

When PCSing (Permanent Change of Station, or moving) to a new area, I always try to incorporate local cuisine and ingredients into my cooking, especially when overseas. Our last home away from yet another home, London, was no exception.

Although when you think of British cooking, you might not always immediately think of dying and going to culinary heaven, I found the local produce to be some of the best in the world. Just mention "Borough Market" to any London foodie and they will immediately tell you *all* the stands you simply *must* hit before you kick the bucket.

In my constant endeavor to feed my children healthy, non-processed food, I signed up for a local farming co-op. I ordered a weekly box of fruit and veggies delivered right to my house. This exposed me to not only ingredients I would never pick out, but some I hardly even recognized. Just Google the word Romanesco and see if you would wonder where and what moment in space-time this green alien became a vegetable.

One of the drawbacks to the farm box was you did get some repeats. By this I mean carrots, bushels of carrots, no, *mountains* of carrots. Lovely as they are, it got to the point that every time I popped the cardboard lid and saw their limp little orange bodies lying at the bottom, my shoulders would droop. I could just hear the children sighing, "carrots and hummus again!?" My dreams started featuring herds of carrots roaming the English countryside.

Suffice to say I learned many new recipes including my constant little companions. Carrot soup, now one of my go-to favorites, is simple, healthy, and quick. Perfect by itself or served with a dollop of plain Greek yogurt and bacon if you're feeling fancy.

Now that we are back in the States, on a cold rainy day there is really nothing more comforting and delicious to take me back to our wonderful time in London.

Carrot Soup

Serves 6

Ingredients:
1 large onion
3 tbsp. butter
2 lb. carrots
2 c. chicken stock
½ c. cream
Ground cumin
Salt and pepper
Fresh parsley, if desired

Kristen Riffle with son Harrison at Borough Market.

Directions:

Coarsely chop onion. In a saucepan, melt butter and sauté onions until soft.

Peel and cut carrots into large chunks. Add carrots and chicken stock to saucepan. Stir.

Bring to boil, reduce to simmer, and cook 20 minutes, stirring occasionally, until carrots can be pierced easily with a fork.

Puree soup in food processor, or use immersion blender.

Add cream and blend. Salt and pepper to taste. Add a dash of ground cumin and fresh parsley as a garnish if desired.

—Kristen Riffle
Army Brat, now Navy wife
Oslo, Norway

Middle East Cuisine Brought Home

I remember sitting in the recruiter's office with my husband, who was my boyfriend at the time. The Marine recruiter asked him why he wanted to join. My boyfriend sat at the desk and lined up blocks listing some of the benefits of military life. He chose "Education" and "See the World" as his top two choices. This was in the year 2000, just before the wars in Iraq and Afghanistan. We had no idea that he would indeed get to spend several years seeing the world. Just . . . not the most savory locations.

In the past sixteen years, he has deployed to Iraq or Afghanistan five times. He also spent several months training in Israel. You might expect that he would return home hating anything that reminded him of combat or the Middle East. Instead, he actually developed an incredible respect for Middle Eastern culture, especially the food. When I learned how to make these sandwiches, we both enjoyed the fresh, light flavors. He said it reminds him of some excellent casual lunches he enjoyed overseas. Apparently, since I haven't sampled a pita sandwich from a Middle Eastern food truck, I haven't truly lived. This is as close as I can get.

I make these about once a week, when I want to lure my husband out of his office and entice him to come home for lunch. Try it! These sandwiches are worth a commute.

Middle-Eastern Chicken Pita Sandwiches

Serves 4

Ingredients:

1 tbsp. white wine vinegar (I have also used red wine vinegar)

2 tsp. olive oil

½ tsp. salt, divided

¼ tsp. black pepper, divided

20 oz. boneless skinless chicken breasts

1 small garlic clove, chopped

1 c. plain Greek yogurt

½ cucumber, shredded, with peel

2 tbsp. chopped mint

4 pita breads

Several leaves of romaine lettuce, chopped

½ small red onion, thinly sliced

Directions:

Marinate the chicken breasts in a Ziploc bag with the vinegar, olive oil, ¼ teaspoon of salt, and ⅛ teaspoon pepper. Squeeze out the air, seal the bag, and knead slightly to coat the chicken evenly. Marinate in the fridge for 2–4 hours.

Make the yogurt sauce by mashing the garlic clove with the flat side of a knife. On the cutting board, mix it with ¼ teaspoon salt and ⅛ teaspoon pepper, until it forms a paste. Stir it into the yogurt in a small bowl, along with the cucumber and mint.

Grill the chicken breasts on medium heat until cooked all the way through, at least 5 minutes on each side. (Discard bag and marinade).

When chicken is fully cooked, cut it into slices.

Top each pita bread with 4 oz. chicken, several spoonfuls of the yogurt sauce, a handful of chopped lettuce, and the sliced red onion.

Enjoy!

—Lizann Lightfoot
Author of the book Welcome to Rota *and*
The Seasoned Spouse Blog: www.SeasonedSpouse.com.

Cajun Debauchery

The story starts out like any good tale involving several Cajuns, a fishing trip, and a few cases of beer. To give some good insight to the creation of this recipe, I have to set up the scene: several members of the Cajun culture, a combination of Swamp and Prairie Cajuns. A distinct difference in the two: Prairie Cajuns are known to put tomatoes in their gumbos, put seasoning on their crawfish, and pronounce pirogue as "pee-row" instead of the proper "pee-rog" as Swamp Cajuns do.

It was decided that a little fishing trip was in order to decide which part of the Cajun culture was the best fishermen. So I, a proud Swamp Cajun (born off the banks of Bayou Lafourche in southern Louisiana), made the trip to the Gulf of Mexico Riviera—Destin, Florida—for a little white sands and spring break debauchery.

We chartered a boat at the local marina and six overzealous LSU students (two Swamp and four Prairie Cajuns) set out in the early hours to bag whatever the Gulf of Mexico offered. A great day of fishing and imbibing occurred, with no clear winner of the Cajun Culture Clash Fishing Tournament. There was much trash talking and even more beer drinking, which cause the participants to forget why we were arguing.

After a great day of fishing, we headed back to the marina with a nice catch of red snapper and triggerfish, along with a couple king mackerel. At the marina, there were photos taken and toasting to a good day with frosty beverages.

The first mate began cleaning the catch as we looked on with celebratory libations. He got to the king mackerel and started complaining on how terrible this fish was to clean and eat, and he wanted to know if we wanted to throw them away. Being Cajuns, we eat any and everything. There is very little we throw away, especially if we caught or killed the game. There IS always a roux, gravy, and/or seasoning you can cook anything in, and it will taste delicious.

We told him he just didn't cook it properly, and he and the boat captain asked us for a good "Cajun" recipe for the king mackerel. Being a white, flaky fish, our fish coubion (most people call it a Courtbouillon) came to mind immediately. Of course, having two different "styles" of Cajun cuisine represented, another heated spirit-induced argument occurred, since each one of our grandmothers had the most amazing recipe which, at that point, was only partially recollected in regard to ingredients and recipe.

We decided the best way to handle the situation was to sit on the dock and write down a good recipe on a bar napkin. What came out of this was a culmination of two Cajun culture cooking concepts fueled by several hours of drinking and hanging out in the sun. Because I was a keeper of the napkin, I was able to attach my last name to the recipe. Also, I hope that the five other participants don't ever see the reproduction of the recipe . . .

Hunter Guidry and his catch, a 32-pound Black Drum (related to the redfish) in Cocodries, LA.

Redfish Coubion (Courtbouillon)

Makes 6–8 servings

Ingredients:

12 pack of beer (one can for recipe, the rest for you)

1.5–2 lb. redfish fillets, diced in 1-inch pieces (you can substitute any firm white flaky fish, but redfish is the best. Especially if you have some bull reds over 27 inches)

1 c. (2 sticks) butter (or vegetable oil—depends on how you like to make your roux)

1 c. all-purpose flour

2 large onions, chopped

2 large green peppers, chopped

2 celery ribs, diced

2–4 garlic cloves (2–3 spoonfuls minced garlic)

2 (14-oz.) cans stewed tomatoes

2 (10-oz.) cans Rotel (spicy if you like it hot, mild for everyone else)

3 (10-oz.) cans tomato sauce

Cajun seasoning (Tony Chachere's)

1 tbsp. sugar

3 green onions, chopped

Jalapeño, diced (for extra spice)

Bunch of parsley, chopped

Hot cooked rice or cooked spaghetti

Directions:

Grab a beer. Prepare the fish. Pull out your big cast iron pot (any large sauce pot will do, but it won't taste as amazing without the seasoned cast iron . . .)

First, you have to make roux! Melt your butter (or oil) on a medium heat and stir in your flour a little bit at the time (some people like a low heat, but it takes a long time).

Cook it to your desired color. I like to do a lighter roux for coubion, so light brownish. Most important thing about a roux is to continuously stir it. Do not walk away. Do not check your phone. Should take about twenty minutes.

Add your "holy trinity" (onion, bell pepper, celery) along with garlic and about half your parsley, and diced Jalapeño.

Cook it down in the roux until it picks up the flavor of the seasoning.

Add in the Rotel, stewed tomatoes, tomato sauce, and a generous amount of Cajun seasoning. I like to cook it down on medium heat for a while to get the flavors going—at least an hour. (This is where the 12-pack comes in handy.)

I would add a lid, so it doesn't bubble molten red sauce all over your stove.

Continually stir the mixture so it doesn't stick to the pot.

At this point, you can taste for seasoning. You can add more Cajun seasoning for spice and a little salt and pepper. Add your tablespoon of sugar at this point as well. Also, if you find the sauce is little thick, you can add a little beer to it.

Add the fish. Return to a boil. Add the green onions and rest of parsley, then stir. Lower the heat to a simmer. Cook for 30 minutes.

Serve over cooked rice*.

*This debate almost stared a ruckus/fist fight on the dock that day. Some believe only in putting the red sauce over rice. Others are more open-minded to putting it over cooked spaghetti. It really depends on your own taste. I can go either way, but I do enjoy it over pasta.

Hope y'all enjoy! Geaux Tigers!!

—Hunter Guidry
Baton Rouge, LA
Nephew of US Navy Capt. (Ret.) Donald Riffle and Beth Guidry Riffle

Pampered Chickens are Delicious

This recipe was given to me by my sister-in-law, Shelly, when she began looking for healthy organic recipes. My brother, Courtney, and I were visiting our dad when Courtney mentioned this fantastic soup. He indicated that he and Shelly were eating a lot of chicken that had been "petted and had their derrieres wiped." Shelly served this soup with organic chicken and used organic chicken broth when making the soup.

Courtney is currently active duty Army stationed at Redstone Arsenal and my dad is retired Army.

Creamy Asparagus and Cauliflower Soup

Serves 6

Ingredients:

1 tbsp. extra-virgin olive oil

3 cloves garlic, minced

1 cauliflower head, cut into small florets

2½ lb. asparagus, trimmed and cut into ½-inch pieces (I like to reserve the flowery tops to add to the soup after blending)

¼ tsp. cayenne pepper

6 c. reduced-sodium vegetable or chicken broth

Salt and freshly ground pepper to taste

Directions:

In a medium soup pot, heat the oil over medium-high heat. Add the garlic and cook for 1 minute. Add the cauliflower, asparagus, and cayenne pepper. Sauté for 4–5 minutes, stirring frequently.

Pour in the broth and bring to a boil. Reduce heat to low and simmer until the cauliflower is fully cooked, 5–8 minutes.

Carefully transfer the soup to a blender and blend on high speed until smooth, about 2 minutes (or use and hand-held immersion blender to puree the soup directly in the pot).

Season to taste with salt and black pepper.

If the soup is too thick, thin it with a little more broth or water. If adding more liquid, return the soup to the stove, bring to a gentle simmer, and heat to the desired temperature.

Serve with a salad and protein of your choice.

—Carrie Woodard
Fairbanks, AK

Spinach Creek Farms, Fairbanks

Alaskan carrots are sweeter due to the cool weather in which they are grown. Carrots specifically from Spinach Creek Farms in Fairbanks are the best! I have the privilege of belonging to this CSA (Community Supported Agriculture) and look forward to receiving the carrots before they are available at the farmer's market.

*The following three recipes really shine when using fresh farmer's market produce.

Spicy Carrots

Serves 6

Ingredients:
6 Alaskan carrots, or the best you can find
¼ c. water
Cayenne pepper
2 tbsp. butter
¼ c. maple syrup

Directions:

Peel and wash carrots. Slice ¼-inch thick on the diagonal so they are oval-shaped flats.

Place the ovals in a large skillet and add water.

Sprinkle with cayenne pepper. A little goes a long way!

Steam the carrots until just beginning to soften.

Add butter and maple syrup. I let them cook a bit longer to allow the syrup and butter to thicken a bit.

Enjoy!

—Carrie Woodard
Fairbanks, AK

Turkey Soup

Thanksgiving is my husband's favorite time of year. He loves turkey. "Please buy the largest turkey, we will eat the leftovers." There are only two of us, even though we have family over on Thanksgiving and send generous portions home, we still have too many leftovers! Nothing can go to waste.

Serves 8

Ingredients:

Leftover turkey meat and carcass
3 or more large onions
6 or more large carrots, peeled
Celery or other fresh vegetables

Fresh or dried herbs: sage, parsley, about 1 tbsp. each dried, handful if fresh
Egg noodles, uncooked

Directions:

Remove all meat from the turkey, and place the carcass in a large pot. Cover the carcass completely with water.

Add half of the onion, carrots, celery, and any other fresh vegetables you may have. These can be left whole or roughly chopped. Add herbs to the pot.

Bring the water up to a boil and then turn down to a simmer. I simmer until I have the chance to deal with it, usually overnight.

Remove the bones, then scoop the vegetables out and discard. Pass the remaining liquid through a strainer to remove all of the overcooked vegetables and meat. We will use only the remaining broth for our soup.

Return the broth to your pot.

Chop the remaining onion, carrots, and celery, and about 4 cups of the leftover turkey. Add to your broth and simmer until the vegetables are tender.

Occasionally, I will add some egg noodles. Be careful not to overcook the noodles (let the directions for timing on the noodle package be your guide).

Salt and pepper to taste. Enjoy!

—Carrie Woodard
Fairbanks, AK

Kale and Avocado Salad

Serves 4

Ingredients (All amounts are approximate):
4 c. kale, torn into bite-sized pieces
1 c. quinoa, cooked
1 c. black beans, drained well
Cherry or grape tomatoes
Sliced avocado
Feta cheese
Fresh lime juice or your favorite citrus dressing

Directions:

Layer all of the ingredients in the order given.

We eat this frequently in the summer as a complete meal on a busy weeknight. My husband will put sliced chicken, turkey, or beef in his if we have any leftover from grilling over the weekend. You know our soldiers cannot do without meat with their dinner. I still haven't convinced him that the quinoa, beans, and cheese provide enough protein.

—Carrie Woodard
Fairbanks, AK

Catfish Dreaming

In 2009–2010, my EOD (Explosive Ordinance Disposal) team was stationed at a tiny outpost in East Baghdad called Zafaraniyah. The four of us were the "bomb squad" for coalition forces operating in the Southeast quarter of town (Karadah to Sadr City and south along the Tigris).

While we had periods of action, some time was spent fighting boredom. As more US forces gradually transitioned into supporting roles, we saw less work. Like most soldiers, we spent a lot of that free time complaining about the food. At the end of the supply line for our region, we were resupplied less frequently than others, and naturally, most of the good stuff didn't make it to us.

There are seven breakfast UGR-A (Unitized Group ration-A) menus and fourteen dinner menus in the Army. I'd say we probably saw a total of seven different meals that year. While that still beats MREs, we went (what seemed like) months with no protein outside of ranch dressing-filled chicken balls.

Although every once in a while, we were lucky enough to get the catfish. We talked about it daily, we scoured the supply trucks coming in to see if we could snag some, and when we did—it tasted better than Thanksgiving dinner. In reality, it probably wasn't all that good, but served as a welcome break from the staples we always had: blueberry muffins, rip-it energy drinks, and Pop-Tarts. This recipe isn't the glorious freeze-dried blackened catfish we had, but given some real ingredients—it's what I would've made.

Catfish Tacos

Serves 4–6

Ingredients:

Peanut/vegetable oil for frying, (about 3 c.)

1½–2 lb. catfish filets, cut into 6-inch strips

Konriko (or your favorite Creole/Cajun seasoning)

2 eggs

2 c. cornmeal

Black pepper

Juice of 1 lime 2 heaping tbsp. mayonnaise

3 tbsp. white vinegar

2 c. shredded red cabbage

1 c. finely shredded white onion

8–10 flour tortillas (6-inch) Cilantro

Tomatoes, coarsely chopped

Hot sauce

Directions:

Fill cast iron skillet with peanut oil to the depth of about 1 inch. Bring oil to 400°F.

Season catfish filets with Konriko.

Beat your eggs in a bowl, and season the cornmeal with black pepper in a separate bowl. Add catfish to the eggs. Mix, ensuring total coverage. Remove fish and coat in cornmeal seasoned with black pepper.

Fry the catfish, about 2 minutes on the first side, and 1 minute on the second side. The coating should be medium brown. Cut open a filet from the first batch to ensure they are fully cooked, adjust timing as necessary.

Prepare the slaw: add lime juice, mayonnaise, and vinegar to a bowl and mix (consistency should be thin). Add shredded cabbage and onion and mix.

Assemble: Warm up tortillas in a dry pan over medium heat, add fish and slaw, garnish further with cilantro, chopped tomatoes, and your favorite hot sauce as desired.

Notes: you can coat/batter the fish in plastic bags and prepare the slaw in another bag to save some dishes. Nice.

—Erik Wood
CPT, US Army

GRANDMA

family

Photo by Steve Dean Photography

PART IV: MORE DIMES THAN DOLLARS
Budget-Minded Meals and Stories

Summertime Delights

During World War II, many staples such as meat, sugar, flour, and butter were rationed. Meat was scarce and of poor quality. Specifically, no steak or prime cut of meat was available. Meatless meals were considered a patriotic duty, and going without showed support for the troops.

On the farm, we raised chickens for meat and eggs, and enjoyed creative dinners all winter, but these ended when the chicken population was reduced to the few hens necessary for egg production. My mother, Ethel Wolf, was the queen of creative cooking, using the most basic ingredients. But by summer, we were ready for a dietary change.

She relieved our dietary boredom with meatless meals using the seasonal crops of strawberries, blueberries, cherries, peaches, and apples: locally grown fruits that conveniently spanned the summer months from June to September. This summertime bounty was prepared as cobblers, shortcakes, and crisps served as the main course.

Warm from the oven, afloat in a bowl of cold milk,
it was summer on the tongue—a blend of sweet, airy dough
with bursts of tart juicy fruit.

Among all these delights, Blueberry Buckle was the favorite that has lasted through three generations of cooks. A buckle is simply cake dough baked with fruit. It is still served (now for breakfast) in Pennsylvania households.

Blueberry Buckle

Serves 8

Ingredients:

¾ c. sugar

¼ c. shortening (wartime oleo/margarine)

1 egg

2 c. sifted flour

½ tsp. salt

2 tsp. baking powder

½ c. milk

2 c. fresh blueberries

Directions:

Preheat oven to 375°F.

Grease and flour a 9-inch pan. Beat sugar and shortening together. Beat in the egg.

In a separate bowl, mix dry ingredients. Add dry ingredients to sugar mixture, alternating with milk.

Lightly toss blueberries with additional flour to coat (keeps them separate in dough). Fold blueberries into batter.

Transfer to a pan and bake for 45 minutes or until lightly brown on top and small cracks appear.

—Pat Brown
Redington Shores, FL

Navy Food

After wracking my brain for three weeks, I finally came up with an answer to Tracey's question: "What makes Navy food unique?"

There were lots of things. Many probably no longer apply—I was in the Navy forty years ago. The most striking thing I recall making a note of at the time was that the Officers' Mess wasn't as good as the Enlisted Mess. I put that down to my having been raised on a farm. Maybe I should've been enlisted, but I wasn't. I still liked to eat with the men.

When I finally settled on a word was the day that I remembered being in a big storm. The ship was rocking and rolling but since I was on an aircraft carrier, it took about twenty seconds for it to roll one way before starting to roll the other. In the mess hall, this created problems—especially for things like soup and coffee. When the ship got to rolling, coffee and soup climbed right out of the cup or bowl and ran across the table like an escaped convict. The solution was to fill the cup or bowl only halfway. But that solved only half the problem.

As you may have heard, Navy ships are kept spotlessly clean. At least that's what we all told mama when we wrote home. Decks and table tops were highly polished, partly to keep the men occupied and partly to keep things from rotting in the sea air.

Putting your bowl of soup down on the table, even when half full, would sometimes result in something called "Split-Pea Shuffleboard." When the ship rolled and reached somewhere around ten degrees, the soup bowl, coffee cup, silverware, and dinner plates would start to scoot from one end of the table to the other. To the credit of some ancient mariner, tables were arranged so that they ran lengthwise perpendicular to the ship's keel. That way, if one did get away, it slid down the table and not into your lap. We call that alignment "athwartships."

Not everyone liked split-pea shuffleboard, so we all put a wet napkin under our cups, bowls, and plates. The napkin wouldn't slide and the dinnerware wouldn't slide off of it.

Problem solved.

Now, I already mentioned the split-pea soup. That was part of the other solution and my segue for telling you the one word I came up with for navy food: thick. Thick soup, coffee that you had to cut with a knife, and no au jus on anything.

—*Thomas R. Cuba*
Author of Dragonfly *by Sebastian Roberts*
"The Political Thriller of 2015"
http://tomcuba.net/dragonfly.html

War Cake:-
2 cups brown sugar.
2 cups hot water
2 table-spoons lard.
1 teas - " salt.
1 " Ground.. Cinnamon
1 " " Cloves
½ pkg seedless raisins.

Boil all above ingredients for
5 minuts after they begin
to bubble.
When cold add:-
1 teaspoon full soda in
1 teas " " Hot water
3 cups Flour beat all together good; bake in slow oven
45 minuts. In 2 loaves.
Swell cake. "Delicious."
Mrs. Weimer
5734 S. Carpenter St.

This is not Navy Food, but a treasured family heirloom that speaks to the WWII Homefront.

Photo by Steve Dean Photography

White Bean and Ham Soup

Serves 8

Ingredients:

1 lb. dry white beans such as great northern (preferred), or navy

1 onion, chopped

3 fresh garlic cloves, finely chopped

2 tbsp. olive oil

1–2 lbs leftover ham/ham bone,

2 qts. (approx.) water *or low-salt chicken broth

1 or 2 bay leaves

Salt and pepper to taste

Fresh spinach and diced tomatoes for garnish, if desired

Directions:

Soak beans overnight, rinse, and drain.

Sauté onion and garlic in olive oil in a large stock pot. Add ham, brown a bit. Add soaked beans.

Cover with water, broth,* or a combination of broth and water, to about 1 inch over beans. Add bay leaves. Bring to boil, then reduce to simmer. Cover and simmer 2–3 hours until meat falls off the bone and beans are tender.

Remove cover if too thin and simmer a while longer.

Mash some of the beans for a creamier texture. Salt and pepper to taste. Garnish with chopped tomatoes and fresh spinach if desired.

*Authors' notes: Also tested using low-salt chicken broth to replace some of the water, and using dried split-peas instead of white beans. All yummy!

Delicious topped with cornbread croutons:

Spread cornbread with butter and chopped garlic.

Cut cornbread to desired size.

Brown in 375°F oven for 15 minutes.

—Don Riffle
Capt. US Navy (Ret.)

Hot Dogs, Again?

My mom and dad married in June, 1960. Dad was enlisted in the Army stationed at Ft. Riley, Kansas. They had a lot of love and very little money to live on. My uncle drove an 18-wheeler and would come through Manhattan, Kansas, and stop to see my parents. He delivered hot dogs for a company and would bring extra packages when he dropped by. Mom and Dad got pretty creative with incorporating hot dogs into their meals.

While I was growing up with my four siblings, we did not eat hot dogs regularly like our friends did. We would ask Mom why. She said she had eaten all of the hot dogs she ever needed during those early lean years of their marriage. I still do not recall a time when I have seen my dad eat a hot dog, although my mom would occasionally enjoy one with just a bit of plain yellow mustard straight from the grill. I do not believe they had a grill in their small apartment in Kansas.

Grilling was the only acceptable way of cooking hot dogs if we ever had them for dinner.

Mom did not care for cooking, although she was a good cook and the five of us kids were always well-fed. Our go-to meal was braised pot roast. That was one of our favorite family meals and what Dad would request whenever he was returning from his many deployments. It is certainly not a gourmet meal, but one that was always served with love.

My dad, Eugene Cote, is a retired helicopter pilot with two tours each in Vietnam and Korea.

Braised Pot Roast

Serves 8

Ingredients (amounts approximate):
5 lb. chuck or other pot roast
2 tbsp. vegetable oil
2–3 lb. potatoes
2 large onions
5 large carrots
1 head cabbage, optional
Salt and pepper

Directions:

Heat vegetable oil in Dutch oven.

Sprinkle roast with salt and pepper. Add to the Dutch oven and sear roast on all sides.

Add water to barely cover. Bring to a low boil, then cover. Reduce heat and simmer on the stovetop for about 2 hours.

About an hour before serving, cut up potatoes, onions, and carrots, and add them to the pot. Quarter the cabbage and add it on top of the roast.

When the vegetables are tender, scoop them into a serving bowl, place the roast on a serving plate, and make gravy out of the meat juices.

—Carrie Woodard
Fairbanks, Alaska

Potato Soup

My husband loves breakfast. Eggs, bacon, and home fried potatoes. On a quiet Sunday morning, I would begin peeling potatoes and put them in a skillet with some oil on the stove, then realize I had more potatoes than two people needed to eat. What do you make when you have peeled too many potatoes? Potato soup to have for dinner later.

Serves 6

Ingredients:

6 potatoes, peeled and chopped
Some of the leftover home fries you made for breakfast (about a cup)
3 leeks, carefully cleaned, or 3 large onions, chopped
Favorite Creole seasoning
1 c. half-and-half or milk

Directions:

Add half of your chopped potatoes to about 3 cups of boiling water and allow them to cook for about 8 minutes. They should be a little softer as this will give the soup its thickness when they "mash" while stirring the soup.

Do not drain cooking liquid.

Add the rest of your chopped potatoes along with the leeks or onions and cook for another 8 minutes, or until potatoes are soft. (Cooking time will vary according to the size of your potato chunks.)

My go-to seasoning is Tony Chachere's Original Creole seasoning. Add to taste, anywhere from 1 teaspoon to 1 tablespoon. It is spicy and salty and gives the potatoes a good flavor.

Right before serving, add the left-over home fries and about a cup of warm half-and-half or milk.

Enjoy.

—Carrie Woodard
Fairbanks, AK

Pensacola Crabbing

Crab lovers accept that they must pay as much per pound as for filet mignon. The sweet, tender meat of this fierce crustacean is lusciously appealing, gentle to the bite, and worth every penny.

Crab on the plate is a celebration. Back when my crab-loving parents were first married, crab was strictly a regional food, and not terribly expensive where you could get it: in Maryland, crab cakes; as she-crab soup in Charleston; tucked in a creole dish in New Orleans; as a feast of huge Dungeness and king crabs in the Pacific Northwest. But for most of the country, crab was simply not available, nor known, nor missed.

My father grew up in Delaware, where his mother served crab cakes for weeknight dinners, sparking his life-long passion for seafood. When his parents, both Georgia natives, moved to Atlanta when he was a teenager, it was a rough transition, and not just because moving inland meant no fresh shellfish.

Dad mourned Delaware, and acted out. My grandparents sent him to college in Abilene, Texas, so that his uncle, a theater teacher there at the time, could knock some sense into him. They did not expect him, at twenty, to acquire a wife. My mother, then eighteen, ate tacos and burritos as everyday foods. To her, fish came from a can.

Dad left college to join the Navy. My mom, who had never known anything but the dry cotton fields of West Texas, went with Dad to Pensacola, Florida, where he was stationed at Corry Field. They rented a one-bedroom cottage, and my mother looked for ways to stretch her meager household budget.

To their delight, Pensacola Bay in the early 1950s was awash in blue crab. This rare treat soon became my parents' sustenance food. "We didn't have to do much of anything," my mom recalled. She had a crab trap that lay flat until the crabs crawled in. It closed when she pulled on a string. She would wade out into the calm, clear bay water and drop the trap, then just pick it up and plop blue crabs into a bucket. The crabs were so plentiful, they seemed only too happy to become dinner.

Mom boiled them whole in water seasoned with Zatarain's Crab Boil, dropping them in one-by-one, head first to kill them quickly so they wouldn't squeak or try to scramble out. The cloves, bay leaf, and allspice in the crab seasoning kept the cottage from smelling of fish.

Then came the task of picking out the sweet, succulent meat. "Those little crabs were tiny," she said. "There wasn't all that much meat in one." She shared the job with other military wives, and the crab-picking time passed fast.

Mom and Dad ate crab once, twice, sometimes several times a week, and Mom savored it just as much as Dad did. "That was a delicacy for me," she said. "I never had anything like that in El Paso." My parents laughed about how much they would miss the crab once his service was up, even though eating it every day made it mundane.

"We got so tired of trying to find different ways to fix it," Mom said. She made crab soup, crab with scrambled eggs, crab on top of salad. Nothing in the cooking she'd learned growing up prepared her for crab, except a croquette, a Southern pan-fried fritter usually made with canned salmon or leftover chicken. She made crab croquettes, and that became her specialty. Croquettes have more filler than a typical crab cake, and no Old Bay seasoning. Mom's croquettes were seasoned with Tabasco, a standard condiment in my

Photo by Hunter Guidry

Blue crabs are no longer as plentiful in Florida, and harvesting is strictly managed. Still plentiful, amusing to watch, and often used as bait, are fiddler crabs. *Photo by Robert C. Neff*

parents' home. A splash of hot sauce found its way into most of Mom's cooking. The crackers added bulk and helped make a meal for a young, hungry sailor.

Mom had one other free-food source: "The guys" who gathered frequently at the cottage to play Tripoley, a combination of hearts, rummy, and poker. The sailors kept all their leftover food whenever the Navy sent them on maneuvers. "Whatever they didn't eat, they brought to me," Mom said. Once, while Mom and Dad were watching a movie on the base, the guys lined up a gift in my parents' Dodge: "We came out, and there was the whole back seat filled with heads of lettuce!" Mom said. "We really had fun. Everybody was young. Those were great times."

Pensacola Navy Crab Croquettes

Serves 6–8

Ingredients:

3–4 dozen blue crabs or 1 lb. blue crab meat, picked over
Zatarain's Crab Boil seasoning
About 10 saltine crackers, crushed
1 large egg, lightly beaten
½ onion, finely chopped
2–3 stalks celery, finely chopped
1 tsp. Tabasco sauce
½ tsp. salt
Oil for frying

Directions:

If using live crabs, boil in water seasoned with Zatarain's Crab Boil for about 10 minutes, until the shells are orange. Pick out all the meat.

Combine cracker crumbs, egg, onion, celery, Tabasco, and salt, then fold in crab meat. Form into patties about the size of a small hamburger.

Put enough oil in a cast iron skillet to fully coat the bottom of the pan. Heat oil so that a crumb dropped into it will sizzle.

Add crab croquettes one at a time, making sure the heat stays at medium high. Cook until golden brown, about 2 minutes on each side.

—Vicki McCash Brennan
Tierra Verde, FL

Celebrate Every Day

Living on an Army Captain's salary in Northern Virginia wasn't easy. My husband Barry, assigned to the Pentagon, daughters Courtney and Whitney, my brother Eric, and I worked to creatively design a life of fun memories on a budget.

We would picnic on the lawn of the Washington Mall, visit the museums, and attend many of the free events offered in the District of Columbia. At home, we took any chance to celebrate.

Each night we set the dining room table, lit candles, and put on soothing music. Often, our young girls would "dress up" with prom-type gowns for dinner and share the day's adventures.

One of our favorite meals was Marinated Flank Steak, wild rice, and fresh vegetables. At the time a flank steak was a cheaper cut of meat that when grilled and thinly sliced would easily feed our family of five. This wonderful recipe was initially shared with Barry, when he was a cadet at West Point, by Major Mark and Patty Hamilton. It has remained a family favorite.

Marinated Flank Steak

Serves 4–6

Ingredients:

¼ c. olive oil
¼ c. soy sauce
2 tbsp. ketchup
1 tbsp. vinegar

¼ tsp. pepper
2 cloves garlic, crushed
Flank steak

Directions:

Combine first 6 ingredients. Pour over flank steak. Cover and refrigerate to marinate for several hours, preferably overnight.

Grill or cook as desired.

Slice thinly across the grain and serve.

—*Gae Bomier*

Rear Guard Cuisine

In late September 1950, during the Korean War, I was seventeen and a corporal in a Battalion Recon team led by Master Sergeant Valentine. We were given a break from the front line duties for about a week before heading through Pyongyang and on to the Yalu River.

Our assignment was to help guard the Kempo airfield near Seoul, South Korea. Upon arrival we were informed that we would only get two meals a day. Full rations were for the forward fighting units.

We had a Korean interpreter assigned to us, called Chang. We took up a collection of American Script and sent Chang to a nearby village to buy food. Chang came back with a big black iron pot, a large bag of rice, and a couple of chickens. Since I was raised on a farm and knew how to clean chickens, I got the job of cleaning the chickens and cooking them.

I cooked the chickens and rice together (no measurements) in the iron pot over an open fire. I stirred the pot with an entrenching tool or bayonet. We all ate, no one complained, no one reported for sick call, and there were no leftovers.

Army Chicken and Rice

Ingredients:
2 chickens
1 bag rice
Water
1 large iron pot

Directions:

Clean chickens. Place in pot with rice and water over an open flame.

Stir with bayonet or other handy tool until done. Recipe feeds 10 hungry soldiers.

(Probably not fit for human consumption.)

—*William B. Terwilliger*
Major, US Army (Ret.)

Helpful Hints from *Victory Cooking*

Vintage, regional cookbooks are a treasure trove for those seeking a glimpse of what life was like in a particular era. This one, from the WWII timeframe, is no exception. Recipes from it have not been included, as few of them would now be prepared as they direct.

It is enlightening, however, for the focus on use of every last available ingredient; for example, there are instructions for preparing stuffed beef hearts (clean carefully, slice open and remove the ventricles) and kidneys, and at least three recipes for homemade bologna.

Here, for both informative and entertainment value, are some of the hints printed in the back pages. Some are still helpful, others are head-scratchers. Some, noted with asterisks (*), should not be attempted, but are nonetheless emblematic of the changes of practices over time:

- Tapioca takes up moisture. A little added to a fruit pie prevents the juice from running out.
- When the egg beater needs oiling, use mineral oil. It is tasteless.
- Hang a pair of tweezers next to the kitchen sink, to be used for pulling out pin feathers in the wings of fowl.
- Do not dry pots and pans over heat. This lazy method is hard on them as the heat is almost certain to warp or crack them.
- Use a whisk broom and warm water for sprinkling clothes. A broom distributes the moisture evenly.
- Use turpentine to remove chewing gum stains. For stubborn grass stains on washable materials, use kerosene and apply by rubbing.*
- Open a can of asparagus at the bottom instead of the top; therefore the danger of breaking the tender tips is eliminated.
- If butter is too hard for creaming with sugar, warm the sugar slightly and the task is simple.
- A fresh egg will sink to the bottom of a dish of cold water.
- Place a peeled apple or a piece of fresh bread in the cake box for additional moisture.
- Put a little butter over the end of a lip of a cream pitcher and it will not drip.
- When cleaning fish, dip the hands in salt so that the fish will not slip, and hold it by the tail.

- Add a little salt to the last rinsing water on wash days and clothes will not freeze when hung out to dry in cold weather.
- Old potatoes won't turn black when boiled, if a teaspoon of vinegar or lemon juice is added to the water.
- Put a spoon in a glass before pouring hot water into it and you prevent it from cracking.
- Eggs should be at least three days old and cold for the best results if the egg whites are to be whipped.
- When putting garments with zipper closings through the wringer, keep the zippers closed and put them through straight. This keeps them in working order, as long as the garments last.*
- Place a piece of charcoal on one of the shelves of the refrigerator. It acts as an absorbent for all odors and purifies the air.
- Before cooking over a picnic fire, rub the outside of utensils with a thin coat of lard. Then soap and water will remove all the black without scouring.

—Provided by Pat Brown
Redington Shores, FL

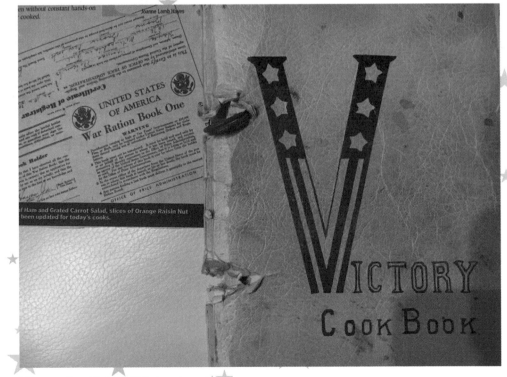

Victory Cookbook, Winterstown, PA.

Resourceful Wartime Housewife

Hunting for rabbits, squirrels, pheasants, quail, and deer was a popular sport in southern York County, Pennsylvania, when I was growing up. The surplus of wild game was a windfall to the housewife preparing meals under trying conditions.

I'm not sure exactly when my mother, Ethel Wolf, acquired a gun and learned to shoot. World War II, with its shortages of meat and rationing may have been the impetus. Or perhaps it was a streak of pioneering spirit to live off the land, which involved canning and preserving everything that would fit in a jar—a patriotic duty to "fight the war on the Homefront."

Whatever the reason, she hunted avidly and successfully every season. Perhaps the quote from her Victory Cook Book sums it up, "Now as never before, meals must be both nutritious and attractive. A little more imagination and originality will not fill the sugar bowl, but they will balance the diet and all the spice that's needed."

—*Pat Brown*
Redington Shores, FL

Ethel Wolf, 1940s, York County, PA.

Authors' note:

Pat Brown did not have her mother's game recipes. The following recipe was provided by Tracey Enerson Wood's nephew, a rising young chef.

Roasted Pheasant with Cabbage Bacon Cream

Serves 2

Ingredients:

2 pheasants, cleaned

Salt, pepper, Old Bay seasoning

¼ c. butter

½ c. raw bacon, chopped

1 sweet onion, chopped

1 celery rib, chopped

2 garlic cloves, minced

3 or 4 sage sprigs, cleaned and chopped

1¼ c. chicken stock

2 c. apple cider

2 apples (Honeycrisp preferred), cored, peeled, and chopped (keep in ice water to keep crisp and prevent browning)

1 head fresh cabbage, rough chopped

⅜ c. heavy cream

Directions:

You will need a large, oven-safe saucepan with lid.

Preheat oven to 375°F.

Season pheasant with salt, pepper, and a dash of Old Bay (cool trick: rub pheasant with mayo before seasoning to create a crispier skin, lock in juices, and the vinegar will help to tenderize the meat).

Melt butter in large saucepan. Place birds in sauce pan and brown all sides. This will take about 5–10 minutes.

Remove birds from pan, and add bacon, onion, celery, garlic, and sage sprigs to the same pan. Cook until onions are soft and bacon is crispy.

Carefully remove any excess fat.

Return the birds to the pan and add chicken stock, cider, and chopped apples. Bring to a simmer, cover with lid, and cook in the oven for 25 minutes, or until birds are fully cooked.

Remove from oven and remove birds from sauce pan (keep birds in oven to keep warm).

On the stove, reduce stock by half, then stir in cabbage. Cook for 3 minutes, then add heavy cream. Continue simmering for a minute or two, add salt and pepper to taste.

Serve pheasant on top of cabbage mixture with mashed or roasted potatoes.

Fried Chicken (Oh My!)

Charles Willard Vannice had achieved the rank of Gunnery Sergeant. Promotions were easy in 1918. He'd lied about his age to join, but that wasn't uncommon in those days. Once in France, he was assigned to a front-line unit and put in charge of a team of men responsible for laying down cannon fire. These teams had to move fast and there wasn't a lot of room to bring along supplies for the daily bivouac. The solution was that rear units would make meals and haul them to the front in a covered truck.

One day his unit was greeted by a dinner truck carrying fried chicken and potatoes. After enjoying a hearty meal, the men all promptly became quite sick. They later learned that the drivers had been attacked with mustard gas.

Determined to fulfill their duty of feeding the soldiers, they had put on their gas masks and delivered the meals to the front lines, not knowing that the gas would leave residuals on the chicken. Gunnery Sergeant Vannice, my grandfather, had stomach problems for the rest of his life.

—*Thomas R. Cuba*
Author of:
Dragonfly *by Sebastian Roberts*
The Political Thriller of 2015
http://tomcuba.net/dragonfly.html

Chicken Paprikash

(This one is edible)

Serves 4

Ingredients:

2 tbsp. butter
2 tbsp. olive oil
2 large onions, coarsely chopped
4 tbsp. Hungarian paprika
4 chicken legs
Salt and pepper
½ c. sour cream

Photo by G. Szenas & D. L. Phelps

Directions:

Heat butter and olive oil in a heavy saucepan until bubbly. Add onions and half of the paprika. Sauté until onions are soft.

Add chicken, spoon onion mixture on top to coat. Cook on medium-high until lightly browned (about 5 minutes). Turn, add the remaining paprika, and cook another 5 minutes. Add salt and ground pepper sparingly.

Spoon onions over chicken. Reduce heat to a slow simmer and cover. Cook for about 1–1½ hours until meat is very tender.

Remove chicken from pan, remove skin. Add salt and pepper to taste.

Stir sour cream into onion pan drippings. Gently bring to a low simmer, do not boil.

Serve chicken topped with the onion sauce. Pairs nicely with German spaetzle.

—Tracey Enerson Wood
St. Petersburg, FL

African Treat

Preparing meals at a remote outstation in Africa without a cook was challenging. It wasn't so remote that we were still living off MRE's, but remote enough that all of our food was flown in via C-130's, and cooking ingredients consisted of mostly dry stores, canned vegetables, and copious amounts of frozen meat. On a really good day we would have a lingering cache of milk and eggs in cold storage.

Everyone fended for themselves for breakfast and lunch, but cooking dinner was a rotating responsibility assigned in pairs. Making dinner could be both enjoyable and a burden; enjoyable when work was slow and you had a good idea and the right ingredients, burdensome when you were busy as hell, and had writer's block for planning a huge meal to feed dozens of impatient, hungry personnel.

Everyone fell into one of two categories when it came to cooking: completely helpless, or fiercely competitive, more so than the most dramatic Food Network cooking show. To combat against the former, most outstations had a simple rule: the cooks voted the worst meal at the end of every week were responsible for cleaning the shitters during weekly camp cleanup. So for the most part dinners were good, and usually protein-rich since everyone spent all free time working out and lifting weights. No meat-free-Mondays here.

Still, most of us were ecstatic when a local national was hired as our cook. Finally, someone to take care of the day-to-day cooking responsibilities and give us more free time. However, there were a few surprises when he arrived: first, he wasn't a very good cook (more of a kitchen assistant), and second, he didn't speak the same language as our resident 'terp (interpreter). So, while we couldn't eliminate the cooking watch altogether, we were able to at least reduce the responsibility to one person per dinner, which halved our collective cooking duties.

The person assigned dinner was still responsible for planning the meal and pulling most of the ingredients, but now he had a helper, an improvised sous chef to compliment the tactical chef. Providing guidance and direction was challenging due to the language barrier, but we made due with a lot of pointing and hand gestures across the kitchen island.

The local cook was also very helpful for the time-consuming prep work and clean up. He didn't mind doing grunt work, was always happy to please, and was often willing to work a bit longer past his scheduled hours in exchange for a tall-boy of the local beer. However, one area where he exceeded our expectations was in the hors d'oeuvre department, in particular, making a classic appetizer, the Samosa.

Samosas are common across Africa, Asia, and the Middle East, and our cook's version of them were relatively simple: sauté some ground meat of any variety, add some spice and vegetables, wrap in bread dough, and fry. They have a distinct triangular shape, and were a delicious snack at any time of day.

Despite the daily grind of the outstation, everyone was a little happier on days when they could walk into the kitchen and there would be a large tray of crispy and delicious Samosas for the taking. They never lasted long. Eventually, we did have to part ways with that cook for some reasons I won't get into here. But even though he's no longer with us, here is his delicious Samosa recipe for others to enjoy.

African Meat Samosas

Makes about 12 appetizer servings

Ingredients:
1 lb. ground beef (or goat, dik-dik, camel, etc.)
1 onion, chopped
2–3 cloves of garlic, chopped
1 c. peas
1 c. diced carrots
1 diced chili pepper
Dash of cumin
Dash of curry
Dash of ginger
Salt and pepper to taste
Chopped parsley or cilantro
Bread dough
Vegetable oil for frying and brushing on dough
Small amount flour and water mixture

Directions:

Cook all the ingredients in a skillet until meat is cooked through. Set to the side.

For the outer dough shell, we typically re-purposed pre-made bread dough from our freezer stores. In order to make this yourself, you probably need some combination of flour, water, and yeast, with a little salt and oil, and then knead it for 20 minutes or so. I'd suggest buying pre-made bread dough.

Once you figure out your dough supply, you want to make softball-sized balls, which you then roll flat into circles approximately a foot in diameter.

Brush each flat piece with a little vegetable oil, then take a knife and quarter it into triangles. Each triangle makes one Samosa.

To build the Samosas, take a dough triangle, and fold the two corners on the curved side to overlap each other, forming a cone shaped cavity. Make sure to mix a little water and loose flour together and rub this mixture on the flat area where the corners overlap so that the seams will stick together.

Spoon the meat filling into the cavity. Fold the last corner over to seal the cavity. Again, be sure to rub the water and loose flour mixture where the corner overlaps to seal the seam.

When finished, the Samosa should look like a small, tight triangular pillow.

Samosas in hotel, Nigeria.

Once you've prepared all of your Samosas, heat up some oil (about ½–1 inch deep) in a skillet to 350°F. Do not crowd the pan; cook in batches if necessary.

Add Samosas, fry, and turn until they are cooked through and have a nice crispy brown on both sides. This will take 5–10 minutes for each batch.

When cooling off, make sure to place them on some paper towels to absorb the excess oil.

Serve with a slice of lemon or lime for garnish, and hot sauce if desired. They will also work well with a chutney sauce if you have any on hand. Use ketchup only if you're desperate . . .

—Scott Riffle
US Navy

PART V: POT LUCK

Dishes Meant to be Shared

Some Like It Hot

We had just moved back to Alaska, after six long years "outside," and were looking forward to seeing my sister and her main squeeze, (now husband) Greg. During the main squeeze phase, we referred to him as "Uncle" Greg, with finger quotes. Why he decided to marry into our family anyway is a story for another book.

Uncle Greg hails from Lafayette, Louisiana, and is a terrific cook, with Cajun and Creole dishes his specialty. Unfortunately, most of the dishes are very time-consuming to prepare, and require ingredients not found in Alaska. So, on visits to the Louisiana relations, Greg brings back a cooler or three of his favorite delicacies: crawfish, boudin, and chicken sausage, all from his favorite supplier, "Best Stop" in Scott, LA . If it had been a good year for fishing in Alaska, the family down south was treated to salmon and halibut, for a happy cooler-content exchange.

Our first requested dish upon his visit to our new quarters at Fort Richardson, was étouffée. He came, toting two coolers and sacks and sacks of groceries, and cooked for us. This may have facilitated the leap from boyfriend to husband from my sister's point of view; my family all love to eat.

During our time "outside" (what Alaskans call anywhere that isn't Alaska) I had acquired a nice collection of bottled hot sauces. Some I bought just because I liked the bottle or the name. One was shaped and painted like a cowboy, and was capped with a little plastic Stetson. Another's label featured a picture of a donkey, and was branded "Dumb Ass." The label featured several blazing red flames and warnings of its excessively hot nature. I proudly showed the collection to Uncle Greg, who tends to like his food spicy. Of course, I also had on hand the more non-hazardous varieties.

I left Greg alone in the kitchen to create his masterpiece, checking back every so often, enticed by the aromas of sautéed garlic, peppers, and onions. He was using his precious stash of Louisiana crawfish, and my mouth watered in anticipation.

Several hours later, when my nose told me the étouffée was nearly done, I snuck back into the kitchen, offering to make the rice. But Greg had things well under control, the rice already in his ginormous rice cooker, ready to go. I noticed the bottle of Dumb Ass open on the counter.

"Greg, you didn't actually cook with this, did you? It's got all these warnings on it." I picked up the bottle, alarmed to see at least an ounce missing.

"Aww, étouffée is supposed to be spicy," he said. "I just used a little bit. It'll be fine."

The table was set, and we all sat down to enjoy the feast Greg had worked all day on. It smelled wonderful, the luscious pink chunks of crawfish perfectly cooked, and swimming in a thick sauce. I stabbed a morsel, brought it to my lips, which burned on contact. Hmmm. I touched the tip of my tongue to a drop of the sauce. Intense burning. I looked up at my husband, who has eaten five-alarm stuff that would have killed me in places like Mexico and Thailand. His face was beet red and sweat was popping out on his forehead.

Greg shoveled in a forkful. "Oh, that's a little hot."

I tried to scrape off the sauce, and at least enjoy the crawfish, but it was no use. Even Greg could not get the ruined étouffée down.

Now, fifteen years later, Uncle Greg never fails to ask if I've got any Dumb Ass Sauce. And for some reason, he no longer cooks in my kitchen when he visits.

—Tracey Enerson Wood
St. Petersburg, FL

Étouffée

Amount depends on the size of the crowd coming over.

Serves 8–16

Ingredients:

Roux:
½–¾ c. Butter
½–¾ c. Peanut oil
1–1½ c. Flour

Veggies:
2–3 large onions, diced (not too small or they just disappear in the gravy)
4–8 stalks celery, diced (you can use the leaves)
1–3 large green bell peppers, diced
4–6 garlic cloves, minced (never enough garlic)
1 stick butter, or 1 c. chicken stock to cook veggies in

Meat:
This depends on the type of étouffée you are making. Since this is seafood, do not add until the last 5 minutes.
2–4 lb. crawfish—with as much crawfish fat you can get (Substitution for crawfish: Halibut, catfish, crab, shrimp, lobster, with the fat from inside the head.)

About 2 qts. chicken stock

Seasoning:
(Do not add "Dumb Ass" hot sauce. All to taste.)
Ground black pepper
Hot sauce—I prefer Louisiana hot sauce
Morton's Season All

Directions:

Making a roux:

Heat a large skillet to medium-high.

Add butter and oil.

When butter is melted, add flour.

*This is very important: stir constantly until the roux has turned to a golden brown.

Remove from heat and continue to stir until mixture cools down. This could take a while, so have a beer.

Making the base for the étouffée:

In a 5–10-quart pot, melt a stick of butter. Never said this was healthy, just that it would taste good. You can substitute a cup or so of chicken stock, if you insist on a healthier version.

Add all veggies and lower heat to medium low. Cover and let the veggies sweat until the onions are translucent and the celery is tender.

Add chicken stock to the veggies, covering them with 2–3 inches of the stock. Raise the heat to medium high and bring to a boil.

Add the roux, making sure you stir, scraping the bottom of the pot to keep it from sticking. Keep stirring for at least 2–3 beers, probably 30 minutes (as long as you don't guzzle).

Add seasonings to the base. Take a taste; it should have quite a kick and lots of flavor.

Continue to add the roux until the mixture is very thick. Not quite a paste, but it should be thick. Lower the heat to medium-low, maybe a little lower. Keep stirring.

Take a taste—the étouffée kick will have decreased quite a bit due to the roux.

Finishing the étouffée:

Now that the étouffée base is mixed, you can add the crawfish or the seafood you want.

This only needs to cook for a few minutes, do not overcook.

Serve over rice with a beer.

—Greg Carmouche
Fairbanks, AK
US Air Force (Ret.)

Gumbo

Serves about 12 (Since I only know how to make a large gumbo)

Ingredients:

Roux:
2–4 c. flour
1–2 c. butter
1–2 c. peanut oil

Veggies:
3–5 large onions, coarsely chopped
1 bunch celery
2–4 large green bell peppers, medium diced
1–3 large red bell peppers, medium diced
1–3 large yellow bell peppers, medium diced
4–6 garlic cloves, finely chopped

Seasoning: to taste
Ground pepper
Parsley
1–1½ tsp. oregano

Now what type of gumbo are you going to make?

Seafood:
2–4 lbs shrimp (peel it before or spend all your time peeling instead of eating)
2–4 lbs crab cut into 1-inch cubes (wow, that is a tough call because you need a lot, so just sell your first-born and get some crab, halibut, or any firm white fish)
2–4 lbs chicken boneless thighs or breasts, cut into 1- to 2-inch pieces

Sausage:
Chicken sausage: 3–5 pounds, cut into 1-inch pieces
(You can try some other chicken sausage but it ain't the same)
Mixed sausage pork and beef 3–5 pounds cut into 1-inch pieces

Chicken stock, preferably homemade, about 2 qts.

Directions:

Make the roux: (see recipe for étouffée). This roux should be much darker than a roux for étouffée. It should be darker than peanut butter. Care must be taken as the roux will burn very quickly at this point. Cool the roux down quickly to stop it from burning or continuing to cook.

Make the base: (see recipe for étouffée)

Once all the veggies are in the base, add oregano and hot sauce. Add the chicken and sausage. Cook until chicken is done.

Continue to cook until you have had 2 beers (remember not to guzzle), 20–30 minutes.

Once the base is complete, add the roux. Stir continuously.

Now add the secret ingredient, homemade chicken stock.

Serve over rice and with a beer.

Note: When making the base, you can make it lower-calorie by using chicken stock instead of butter. By using chicken stock, it is also easier to stop it from sticking.

—*Greg Carmouche*
Fairbanks, AK

Greg Carmouche with daughter Emily Scarmuzzi, Fairbanks, AK, 2015.

Jambalaya

This can be done several ways to change the flavor.

Serves 12–16

Ingredients:

What type do you want to make? Chicken, Shrimp?

Meat:

2–3 lb. chicken thighs (boneless), cut into 1-inch pieces, or

2–3 lb. large shrimp, cut in half

1–2 lb. sausage: (Andouille), sliced lengthwise, then into half-inch pieces

Peanut oil: enough to cover bottom of stock pot

Veggies:

1 large onion, diced

2 stalks celery, diced

1 large green bell pepper: (regular jambalaya) *or*

1 large red bell pepper (red jambalaya), diced

3 garlic cloves, minced

½–1 lb. tomatoes for red jambalaya, fresh or canned, diced

Chicken stock—¼–½ c.

1 can spicy V8

Rice: amount depends on how much you like rice; this is easiest if cooked ahead

3–4 c. yellow or saffron rice for regular jambalaya,

White or brown rice for red jambalaya

Seasonings:

Black ground pepper as desired

1½–2 tsp. oregano

1½–2 tsp. thyme

Your favorite hot sauce

Directions:

Let's start cooking. This does not have a roux, so omit that step.

Add some peanut oil into a 5–8 quart stock pot. Add chicken and cook until browned, then set aside.

Add sausage and brown, then set aside.

Add veggies and cook until tender. Now here comes the curve ball. Is this a red or yellow jambalaya?

Yellow jambalaya? Okay, let's do that first:

Add the meat back into the pot. Unless you are using seafood, then wait a minute. Add some chicken stock, about ¼ cup or less. Make sure to bring to a quick boil and scrape the bottom to remove the tasty goodness there.

Remember, you can add more chicken stock if needed.

Add the yellow/saffron rice to the pot (that you cooked ahead of time, right?) stirring and adding more chicken stock, but not reducing to a mush. You want the rice to be moist.

If this is a seafood jambalaya, rice should be a little dry. Add the shrimp and cook for 5 minutes.

Now for the red jambalaya, which is more of a tomato base then the yellow:

Add the meat back into the pot. Hold off if you are using seafood. At this point you may like some tomatoes, so dice up 1 or 2 (or add a can or two of diced). Cook until they are tender.

Add some chicken stock, about ¼ cup or less. Make sure to bring to a quick boil and scrape the bottom to remove the tasty goodness there. You can add more chicken stock if needed.

Add the rice (that you cooked ahead of time) to the pot, stirring and adding spicy V8 to it. How much V8, you ask? *shrugs shoulders* I don't know. You're an adult, figure that stuff out; I did.

Remember, do not stir so much you turn it into a mush. If it is a seafood jambalaya, add the seafood now, stir, and cook for 5 minutes.

This concludes cooking with Greg.

Oh yeah, add your own special ingredient, such as hot sauce, anytime you want to.

And of course the chicken stock is homemade and takes 2 days to make so I guess that may be a little special.

—*"Uncle" Greg Carmouche*
Fairbanks, AK

When in Spain . . .

One of the highlights of my husband's military career was when we were stationed in Spain for three years. He was lucky to receive accompanied orders to Naval Station Rota, Spain! Our family had an amazing time exploring the local culture and eating lots of Spanish food. I even made some Spanish friends who welcomed us to their family gatherings.

In Spain, paella is the official party dish for large family events. It is cooked outside in giant pans over a fire. The recipe for paella differs in every region in Spain, depending on the regional specialties. Because we lived in Southern Spain, in a fishing town, the local paella was made with various kinds of seafood and snails. It could even include squid ink, which turned the rice black!

However, I learned that seafood paella is difficult to reproduce in the States because of limited fresh seafood in many supermarkets. In addition, it is more cost-effective to include some cheaper meats, like chicken thighs. So, I adapted this version as *my* paella recipe. I have served it to American and Spanish friends, and they all loved it! It is featured in my book *Welcome to Rota*, which is a guidebook for military families living in Southern Spain.

All the ingredients can be found in America. Saffron is expensive, but necessary to prepare any paella dish. Paella rice, Bomba, is a short-grain rice similar to Arborio, which is used in risotto. Finally, you will need a large paella pan. No need to cook over an open flame outside though—this recipe is prepared on the stovetop.

Meat and Seafood Paella

Serves 8

Ingredients:

Olive oil

1 lb. chicken thighs, boneless and skinless

1 lb. chorizo sausage

1 c. green beans or peas

3 fresh tomatoes, peeled and seeded

2 onions

1 red bell pepper

2–3 cloves garlic

3¾ c. chicken broth

1 generous pinch saffron

Smoked paprika, salt, and pepper to taste

1¾ c. paella rice (Bomba or Arborio)

1 lb. shrimp, fresh or frozen, with tails on

½ lb. clams or mussels

Optional garnishes: lemon wedges, parsley, and chopped green olives

Directions:

Chop all vegetables and meat.

Put a few tablespoons of olive oil in a large paella pan (or whichever large pan you have available) over medium-high heat. Cook the chicken, chorizo, and vegetables until the meat is brown and the onions and peppers are soft.

Add all the chicken broth, a large pinch of saffron, salt, pepper, and smoked paprika to taste. Bring to a boil.

Once the pan is boiling, add all the rice. Stir it around *once*, then cook over medium high heat for 20 minutes without stirring.

Every few minutes, rotate the pan on the burner so the wide pan can cook evenly. Continue rotating until all liquid is absorbed.

Meanwhile, cook the seafood by steaming it in a large covered pot over boiling water for about 5 minutes. Make sure all clams or mussels have opened, and ensure that shrimp is completely pink. Toss or stir at least once to get even cooking.

When paella is cooked, arrange seafood on the top, along with green olives, parsley, and lemon wedges.

Cover with a clean towel and allow to cool for a few minutes so flavors can blend.

Serve with red wine for an elegant meal.

—Lizann Lightfoot
Author of Welcome to Rota *and* The Seasoned Spouse
Blog: www.SeasonedSpouse.com.

My Favorite Recipe

My name is John Schmermund and I served in the 301 OMS (SAC), Lockborn Air Force Base, Columbus, Ohio, starting in 1970. I was a Crew Chief on a KC-135, inflight refueling tanker.

My favorite recipe is called Green Shrimp. It was a family tradition on the Schmermund side of the family, to have during holidays and birthdays. The family would order large (15/20 count) frozen shrimp in five-pound boxes to be shipped to Grandma and Grandpa Schmermund's residence in Ohio.

John, Joann, and Anna Schmermund with author Tracey Enerson Wood.

Green Shrimp

Five pounds would feed about four adults. You need at least a 6-quart steamer that can hold five pounds of unpeeled shrimp in the basket.

Ingredients:

4 cans beer, such as Shiner Bock
1 pt. prepared mustard
1 c. apple cider vinegar
10 tbsp. salt
4 tsp. black pepper
4 tsp. cayenne pepper
4 tsp. celery seed
4 tsp. whole allspice
5 lb. (15/20 count) unpeeled shrimp

Directions:

Bring all ingredients except shrimp to a low boil in the bottom part of a steamer pot.

Place shrimp in the basket. You need to steam (only steam, no shrimp should rest in slowly boiling ingredients) the shrimp slowly.

Baste every 15 minutes by pouring the boiling liquid over all the shrimp in the pan, then return to the heat. This process goes on for 2 hours.

Shrimp is to be served hot with guests peeling their own.

Serve shrimp along with homemade baked beans and potato salad. Garlic bread with beer to drink works well.

You can cook 10 pounds of shrimp in a 10-quart steamer the same way.

I hope you enjoy our family recipe of Green Shrimp as much as all my family and friends have over the last 80 years.

—*John Schmermund*
Louise, TX

Kitchen Wars

My family has taken to holding a *Chopped* television show-style cooking competition whenever we get together, and we're pretty competitive—well, competition is waning now, as I've never lost. So with this recipe I'll offer some pro-tips if you ever find yourself in a cooking competition.

The secret ingredients on this particular day were eggplant and shrimp.

Tip# 1: Ingredient recon: Before the competition, if it's not your kitchen, look through everything to ID good ingredients and develop a couple themes for where you might take your recipe. If it's your kitchen, hide the good stuff.

Tip # 2: Have a starch identified—save some time by picking a couple of potential containers (tortilla, puff pastry, egg roll wrapper, noodles, bread) to contain the secret ingredients. Obviously they won't always be appropriate; in this case, I was going grilled cheese all the way after finding five cheeses in recon.

Tip # 3: Clock management. One of your ingredients likely takes significantly longer to cook than others. Start that process first, then move on to the complicated mixes/chopping/etc.

Tip # 4: Dipping Sauce—people love dipping their food, so if you have a sauce, don't apply it, let them do it.

Tip # 5: Don't make a low-fat/low-carb/gluten-free/free rangin' item for a competition. Save the "healthy" options for the losers. Bacon? Yes. Deep-fry? Yes. Steamed lentils? No. Leave that trash alone.

Three-Cheese Shrimp Toasts

Serves 8 as appetizer

Ingredients:

1 loaf french bread

2–3 tbsp. olive oil

Peanut/vegetable oil (enough to cover bottom of pan)

1 lb. shrimp, peeled and deveined

3 cloves garlic, crushed

½ lb. eggplant, thinly sliced

A few pinches each of salt and black pepper

½ lb. shredded cheese—any mix of provolone, mozzarella, and Parmesan

½ c. mayonnaise

⅓ c. sriracha sauce

1 tsp. lemon juice

Directions:

Prepare the toast: slice the loaf into ½-inch pieces diagonally, brush both sides with olive oil and put in the oven at 400°F for 2–3 minutes (don't dry them out completely, you want to retain some chew).

Pan fry the shrimp: bring peanut oil to 400°F, and add shrimp and crushed garlic. This should take about 50 seconds total—don't overcook, and remove from pan immediately to cool (they will continue to cook internally).

Brush the eggplant slices with oil and lightly salt/pepper. Add to oven at the same time; it should take about 10 minutes to soften up sufficiently.

Prepare dipping sauce: add mayo, sriracha, and lemon juice to a serving bowl and whisk.

Assemble: leave toasts on cookie sheet, place eggplant first and then shrimp onto toasts and cover generously with cheese (to hold the shrimp on). Place back in oven at 400°F for a couple minutes to melt the cheese.

Remove and arrange on serving dish. Reign victorious and hear the lamentations of the defeated.

—Erik Wood
CPT, US Army

Qatari Challenge

I don't really have stories about food that end in a good way . . . warm camel milk straight from the udder with hair floating on top was an unfortunate experience in Riyadh a few years back . . . or eating the fat from a baby camel's hump at an Emirati prince's falcon ranch . . . you get the idea. Anyway, the story below was pretty funny and one I'll remember for a while.

One of my duties was to lead the multi-disciplined security teams that were deployed to provide force protection during major exercises in theater. My teams consisted of military police, explosive ordnance disposal teams, K-9 units, counter intelligence and counter surveillance personnel, and some other specialties.

In 2007, Exercise EAGLE RESOLVE '07 was being held in Doha, Qatar. The Qatari Chief of Security and my counterpart, Colonel Mohammed, was an exceptionally outgoing character and a very gracious host. One way to ensure the success of these missions was to develop a close relationship with our host nation counterparts. It was therefore very important to take every opportunity to engage in cultural and social interaction.

One afternoon Colonel Mohammed invited my senior intelligence and military police officers and me to an informal lunch in his office with his senior staff. When we arrived, the area on the floor in front of his desk had been cleared and there was a shiny silver platter roughly three feet in diameter, laid on a large area rug.

The platter held a complete, cooked goat set over a bed of rice. The food smelled amazing but I have to admit, the goat was a pretty scary sight. I was happy the cooked skull (with eyeballs intact) was not facing directly toward me.

Our host alternated the Americans and the Qataris as we sat on the floor around the platter. Colonel Mohammed gave a brief welcome, I responded with thanks, and it was time to eat. Tradition is that you only use your right hand when taking food from the platter as the left hand is reserved for other "unclean" activities. We pulled strips of greasy meat and handfuls of rice squeezed into balls from the platter and shoveled the food right into our mouths. The flavor was amazing and our host could tell we were enjoying the lunch. This is where things went south.

During interaction among military members, there is often some rivalry and hazing that occurs as relationships are built. The officer in charge of my military police detachment, Joseph, had established a reputation as a pretty tough customer, but the Qataris were intent on taking him down a notch.

They wanted him to have the full goat dining experience so he was first offered one of the goat's testicles. He obviously wasn't too excited, but our hosts explained that they were very nutritious, were known to improve virility, and tasted like chicken. He managed to get one down followed by a quick gulp of water. Joseph had tipped his hand though, and the Qatari's knew they were on the right track.

Next came an eyeball. Joe opted for the swallow-it-whole method in getting this down, but I'm pretty sure I saw a little bit of gag reflex toward the end. I have to give him credit though, he had graciously accepted the offer (challenge) and eaten the eyeball without losing it.

Finally, Colonel Mohammed's Chief of Staff pulled the skull of the goat in front of him and grabbed the upper and lower jaws of the goat and cracked the lower jaw off. Using two fingers on his right hand he reached in through the now exposed underside and scooped out a lump of cooked brain. It looked like grey lumpy pudding. I could see fear in Joe's eyes. The Chief of Staff handed him the "pudding" and Joe looked at for a few seconds, gave it a smell, and shoveled it in (I don't think he should have smelled it).

He held on for a second but couldn't work up the resolve to swallow it. He jumped up and headed out the door with the pudding still in his mouth. Before Joe had even crossed the threshold, the Qatari's were laughing so hard they couldn't speak. While Joe was still out of the room finding a place to deposit his bite of brains, the Qatari's explained that they never eat the brains or the eyes; the texture and flavor are not very appealing. It was a tradition and necessity from the Bedouin days that had been abandoned as more culinary choices became available after the Middle East oil and natural gas windfalls.

The Qataris had won this round. Joe was a little more humble and managed to dodge all the other luncheons in Colonel Mohammed's office.

—Sean W. Haglund
Deputy Chief, Chemical, Biological, Radiological and Nuclear Requirements Support
Washington, DC

Author's note: *Mr. Haglund has no recipe from his Qataran feast. The following recipe for Spring Rolls is a much-demanded treat at local gatherings, wherever the location, and easily adapted to local ingredients.*

★ ★ ★ ★ ★ ★ ★ ★ ★ ★ ★ ★ ★ ★ ★

Photo by Steve Dean Photography

Spring Rolls

Makes about 15 rolls

Ingredients:

½ lb. ground beef

½ lb. ground pork, Italian sausage, venison, moose, turkey, caribou, or other available protein

1 small onion, chopped, or 4 large scallions, thinly sliced

1 c. mushrooms, thinly sliced

1–2 tbsp. chopped garlic

1–2 c. dried mung bean thread, or Napa cabbage, or other vegetables, carefully cleaned, finely chopped

3 tbsp. soy sauce

1 tbsp. ground black pepper (omit or reduce if using hot Italian sausage)

½ tsp. sesame oil (optional)

2 eggs, lightly beaten

1 pkg. egg roll or lumpia wrappers*

Vegetable oil for frying

Dipping sauces as desired

Lumpia wrappers have a nice, flaky/crunchy texture, but are harder to work with.

Directions:

In a pan over medium heat, brown the meat, breaking any large chunks to make a consistent, small crumble. Drain and set aside to cool.

Sauté onions and mushrooms until soft, add garlic, and sauté until fragrant, about one minute. Add to meat mixture.

Blanch mung bean threads, cabbage, or other vegetables in boiling water, about one minute. Cool, then mix into meat mixture. Add soy sauce, other seasonings, and half of the eggs.

Place vegetable oil in deep fryer, or frying pan to depth of 1 inch. Heat to 350°F.

To wrap: take one egg roll wrapper at a time and lay it on flat surface. Place a heaping tablespoon of meat mixture onto the wrapper, about a third up the wrap.

Roll up from bottom, until about ⅔ up wrap. Dip finger into remaining beaten egg, run along sides and top, then fold each side toward center. Roll up remainder and press together gently to seal.

Fry, turning if not using deep fryer, until golden brown. Remove and drain on rack or paper towels.

Enjoy with sweet and sour and soy sauce. May be frozen up to three months.

—Tracey Enerson Wood
St. Petersburg, FL

G-String Progressive Dinner

The G-String (see page 34) invited me to join them for lunch at a local restaurant. As I was the only one who worked outside the home, the three of them were already deep in conversation when I arrived.

We had previously shared many adventures and misadventures, and they wasted no time in filling me in with the latest of their schemes. "We want to have a progressive dinner when the guys redeploy. The chief, our spousal units and us, maybe the general and his wife if they want to come. We start at one house, then move on to the next for each course."

I was still processing the logistics of this when Janet piped in, "I'll make the dessert!"

Melody countered with "I'll make a salad."

Julia added, "We can start with an appetizer at my house."

I had been effectively ambushed. All eyes turned to me, and I offered the only remaining piece. The main course. For eleven people. Including my husband's boss, and boss's boss. Served in my home after first running around to two or three other homes. On a Friday after work. No problem.

The event was a great success. I made a beef tenderloin that I stuffed and tied the night before, and popped in the oven before heading out for the first course, praying it would be done in time. I snuck back early to check on it, only to find my husband's boss had beaten me to it. He was in my kitchen, sawing off chunks of tenderloin, and working my pepper grinder to its limits. "Mmm. Good. I like pepper." He opened up the grinder and poured a heap of whole peppercorns onto another forkful.

Stuffed Beef Tenderloin

Serves approximately 3–4 people per pound

Ingredients:

2 c. carrots, peeled and julienned
2 large onions, chopped
1 root vegetable, such as turnip, yam, or parsnip, peeled and chopped (optional)
Vegetable oil
1 beef tenderloin (trim off excess fat and the silver membrane)
Salt and pepper

Directions:

Sauté vegetables in small amount of oil until crisp-tender. Season to taste with salt and pepper.

Slice the tenderloin lengthwise, beginning and ending about 2 inches from both ends, but not all the way through, creating a pocket.

Stuff the sautéed vegetables into the pocket, and secure by tying with butcher string.

*This may done a day in advance and refrigerated.

When ready to cook, preheat oven to 425°F.

Brown the tenderloin in a large hot skillet with a small bit of oil, turning to brown sides.

Roast, uncovered, in oven until meat reaches your desired doneness. Check with meat thermometer. I remove at 125°F for rare to medium rare, which takes 30–50 minutes, depending on size.

Let sit 15–20 minutes before carving.

Salt and pepper to taste.

—Tracey Enerson Wood
St. Petersburg, FL

Come as You Are!

When my husband, Barry, was promoted to Major, we celebrated with a house party.

Living in Burke, Virginia, outside of DC, most people were accustomed to formal receptions and dinners. However, we were both raised in the Midwest town of Flint, Michigan, where a typical gathering was very casual. So our invitations suggested that guests wear "Michigan casual" clothing—jeans, flannel shirts, sweaters, etc.

Our menu was equally casual and very hometown: Coney Dogs like those featured at Angelo's Coney Island, Vernor's Ginger Ale, and beer. Most of our guests were unfamiliar with the taste of steamed Koegel hot dogs, smothered in the wonderful, spicy sauce. The dogs were topped with chopped onion and mustard. Mmmmmmmm!

Although we had prepared an ample amount of Coney sauce, we ran out early and needed to cook up a new batch.

Coney Island Hot Dogs

Approximately 20 servings

Ingredients:

1 tsp. shortening

1½ lb. ground beef

2 medium onions, finely grated

6 oz. tomato sauce

½ tsp. garlic powder

6 oz. water

2 tbsp. chili powder

1 tbsp. prepared mustard

4–5 hot dogs, ground (preferably Koegel Vienna's)

20 hot dogs and buns

Additional chopped onions and mustard

Directions:

Brown ground beef in shortening, then drain.

Combine next 7 ingredients with beef. Simmer until thick.

Serve on top of hot dogs with more mustard and chopped onion.

—Gae Bomier

Photo by Steve Dean Photography

A Watched Pot

As time went on and my husband had been promoted a few times, I had many years to learn to entertain and be comfortable with myself as a host and could cook a few meals.

Jim had a Division Command at Fort Drum, New York. We had been there a very short time when he was deployed to Bosnia. The current Chief of Staff of the Army was then General Eric Shinseki, and his wife, Patty, was coming to visit the spouses.

I hosted a gathering of Senior Spouses: General's, Colonel's, and Lieutenant Colonel's wives. At that time of his career the army would offer me some assistance in the kitchen, but I insisted that I could handle a meal. I chose a casserole that had been served to me by one of the previous Division Commander's wives, Francie Meade. I had prepared it a number of times and was quite confident I could handle this casserole, salad, and dessert.

Mrs. Shinseki was a gracious woman and I was at ease with her. Well, she arrived and the ladies were all enjoying meeting her. I was in the kitchen and all I had left to do was boil the noodles. But—I could not get the extremely large pot of water to boil! Everyone was so nervous for me, it was almost comical.

One of the other general officer's wives offered to go home and boil water and other wives were wringing their hands a bit. It was getting tense as I was on my first test from the new group of ladies at Fort Drum.

God willing and the creek did not rise . . . my water came to a boil and we managed to eat before everyone had had too many snacks. We all had a good laugh and enjoyed our meal together.

Cavatini

Serves 16

Ingredients:

2 lb. ground beef

1 lb. ground pork or Italian sausage

1 (7 or 8-oz.) pkg. sliced pepperoni

2 small cans mushrooms (about 7 oz. each) drained, or 16 oz. sliced fresh mushrooms

1 onion, diced

1 green pepper, diced

2 (32-oz.) jars Prego spaghetti sauce

Salt and pepper to taste

12 oz. pasta such as mostaccioli or rotini, cooked according to package directions

Shredded mozzarella cheese to cover top, about 2 cups

Directions:

Over medium heat, brown the ground beef and sausage with onion, green pepper, and mushrooms. Drain fat.

Add pepperoni and sauce and simmer one hour.

Add cooked noodles, and combine. Transfer to large oven-proof casserole dish or two 9x13 baking pans.

Top with cheese. Bake 10–15 minutes at 400°F.

Can be frozen.

Recipe from Francine Meade, 1993
Submitted by Carol Campbell
Wife of LTG (Ret.) Jim Campbell

LTG Jim Campbell and Carol Campbell, 2006.

No Soup (Spoon) For You!

My last story is from when my husband had made his third star and he had an enlisted aide, Master Sergeant David Turcotte. The aide worked in our home during the day and assisted when we had official entertaining. We were living in Hawaii and were stationed at Fort Shafter.

I was on the Armed Services YMCA board and I hosted the group of twenty or so for lunch. Master Sergeant Turcotte prepared a lovely meal. The first was a soup course. He always loved his Gazpacho recipe. I had become accustomed to him helping, as he had been with us for a couple of years, and did not check the table.

We were all seated at our dining room table that could accommodate twenty-two! A long table to say the least, and I was still adjusting to its formality and enormous proportions, and the expectations that went along with it. Somehow I needed to make it fit into my casual style of entertaining.

One of my guests said, as she picked up her spoon, "This is an interesting way to eat soup!" We had put out the iced tea spoons instead of the soup spoons. I just laughed and told her we liked to challenge our guests! We laughed about that many times and once again, found humor to be the answer.

LTG Jim Campbell at promotion of SFC David Turcotte, Fort Meyer, VA, circa 2006.

Gazpacho

Serves 6–8

Ingredients:

1½ lb. vine-ripened tomatoes, peeled, seeded, small diced

1 c. cucumber, peeled, seeded, small diced

½ c. red bell pepper, small diced

½ c. red onion, small diced

1 small Jalapeño, seeded, minced

1 medium garlic clove, minced

¼ cup extra-virgin olive oil

1 lime, juiced

2 tsp. Worcestershire sauce

½ tsp. ground cumin, toasted in oven at 250°F for 8 min.

2½ tsp. good balsamic vinegar

1 tsp. kosher salt

12 oz. V8 juice

¼ tsp. freshly ground black pepper

6 oz. sour cream (optional)

2 tbsp. fresh basil leaves (optional)

1 tsp. hot sauce (optional)

Directions:

Combine all ingredients in a large mixing bowl.

Transfer 1½ cups of the mixture to a blender and puree for 15–20 seconds on high speed.

Return the pureed mixture to the bowl and stir to combine. Cover and chill for 2 hours minimum, but not more than 18 hours.

Heat may be adjusted with hot sauce.

Serve with sprig of basil and a dab of sour cream.

—Recipe by MSG David Turcotte, CEC, AAC/Enlisted Aide to LTG Jim Campbell
Submitted by Carol Campbell
Wife of LTG (Ret.) Jim Campbell

Key West Tacky Cookie Jar Club

Beth's Eclectic Chocolate Chip Cookies were developed during my husband's joint command tour in Key West, Florida. Life was quite idyllic during that time, with neighbors and friends gathering almost daily to toast sunsets on the pier *du jour*.

With our first Christmas in the Keys approaching, I wanted to create a fun gift for new friends and neighbors that reflected the Key West ambiance of tropical fun with a splash of tacky—also a local trait. I painted flamingoes on cookie jars and found delightful matching ornaments to tie to them.

Next, I had to decide what culinary treat to put in the jars. I experimented with a basic cookie dough recipe, adding and substituting ingredients, then baking and taste testing—this went on for a few weeks. Bob, a neighbor and now longtime friend, was a willing taste-tester, during which time he gained several pounds.

The recipe evolved as his taste buds approved, finally arriving at *the* eclectic cookie recipe. I filled the tackily painted jars with the resulting big cookies and the tacky cookie jar club was born.

There are about eight editions of tacky jars over the years, and who knows, one day I might start these up again. In the meantime, no matter what the cookies are served in, they are a big hit. It is a fact that in the halls of the Pentagon, most know me as that gray-haired lady who makes the big cookies for the holiday parties.

Beth's Eclectic Chocolate Chip Cookies

Makes about 32–36 cookies

Ingredients:

2¼ c. all-purpose flour

1 tsp. baking soda

1 tsp. salt

1 c. (2 sticks) butter, softened

¾ c. packed light brown sugar

¾ c. sugar

2 large eggs

1 generous tbsp. vanilla extract

11- or 12-oz pkg. semi-sweet chocolate chips

11- or 12-oz pkg. milk chocolate chips

11- or 12-oz pkg. white chocolate chips

1½ heaping cups pecans (broken, not finely chopped)

1½ heaping cups walnuts (broken, not finely chopped)

Directions:

Preheat the oven to 325°F.

Whisk together flour, baking soda, and salt, and set aside.

Beat butter (real butter) with sugars, then add eggs and vanilla and beat until real fluffy. Slowly add flour mixture, beating well after each addition.

In a very large bowl, mix chips and nuts together. Plop cookie dough on top of nut and chip mixture and mix well.

Pack ice cream scoop full to form cookie. Drop onto cookie sheet with enough space for cookies to spread a bit.

Bake at 325°F for 25 minutes. You may have to tweak cooking time depending on your oven's individual quirks!

Let cookies sit on the cookie sheet for about 2–3 minutes after coming out of the oven to "set" a bit—they are large and will be very malleable. Remove from cookie sheet to wire cookie rack to cool thoroughly.

Enjoy!

Notes:

These cookies take a bit longer to prepare and bake. Because of their size, the oven temperature is lower and baking time is longer. If you decrease the size of the cookie, you may need to adjust the baking time accordingly.

It will seem as though there isn't enough cookie dough to cover all of the chocolate chips and nuts, but there is! *Really!* I find it easier to mix the nuts and chocolate first, then "plop" the dough on top to begin mixing. You may need to get your hands into it or use heavy mixing spoons—have fun!

I don't chop the pecans and walnuts, but break them into chunks—just a personal preference to make the cookies really "chunky!"

Allow the eggs and butter to warm up to room temperature.

I use a rounded medium sized ice cream scoop (#20) to scoop out the finished cookie dough onto air bake cookie sheets. You can use a larger or smaller scoop, but may have to tweak your baking time a few minutes.

—Beth Guidry Riffle
Alexandria, VA

Photo by G. Szenas & D.L. Phelps

Wedding Cake

When my son, an active duty Army officer, was about to marry our wonderful daughter-in-law, things were hectic. He was consumed in pre-deployment training in another state, and she was juggling a full-time job and planning their move overseas. They wanted to keep their wedding simple, fun, and personal, in reflection of their values and time constraints.

There was to be no wedding cake. Now, I try to be a supportive, non-judgmental parent of adult children, offering advice when asked and otherwise keeping my big mouth shut. I said I try, I'm not always successful.

In this case, I really wanted a cake, believing the whole thing would be somehow incomplete without one. So I offered to order and pay for the cake, have it delivered, etc., if they would allow it. The bride and groom graciously accepted my offer, even though I explained that my vision called for a rather non-traditional cake. In fact, I pictured a topsy-turvy cre-

This is the result.

ation, with layers reflecting their lives before marriage (they are both military brats, and grew up all over) and topped with a road map of their future adventures.

I was pretty proud of it, and think it was a hit.

When it comes to having adult, and even small children, it is important to figure out when you are helping and when you are interfering. Sometimes, even if every bone in your body tells you that your child is taking the wrong path, you have to shut up and let them. If there is no threat of imminent bodily harm, it is probably best to let them learn their own lessons.

But sometimes, it's just a cake.

Coconut Cake

Serves 6–8

Ingredients:

Batter:
4 oz. (one stick) stick butter, softened
1 cup granulated sugar
2 eggs
2 tsp. vanilla extract
1½ c. self-rising flour, sifted
½ c. coconut milk

Filling:
½ c. coconut cream
¼ c. coconut milk
1 tsp. lemon juice
1 tsp. lemon zest (optional)

Frosting:
8 oz. cream cheese
2 oz. butter, softened
¼ c. coconut cream
1 c. confectioners' sugar, sifted, more or less
   to taste
Lemon zest (optional)
8 oz. sweetened coconut flakes

Directions:

Preheat oven to 350°F.

Grease and lightly flour two 8-inch round non-stick cake pans.

Batter: cream butter and sugar together, then beat until fluffy. This is easiest in a stand mixer, as it will take several minutes.

Beat in eggs and vanilla extract.

At low speed, add in half of the flour, then half of the coconut milk, then the rest of the flour. Add the remaining coconut milk and beat another minute.

Bake for 20–25 minutes, or until the cake springs back when touched, or toothpick in center comes out clean. Set aside to cool, then remove from pans.

Mix filling items. When cake is cool, poke all over each layer with a skewer. Pour half the filling on each layer. Let sit for at least an hour for filling to absorb.

Frosting: Beat cream cheese, butter, and coconut cream at medium speed, until fluffy. Beat in most of the confectioners' sugar, then taste. Add sugar until you reach desired sweetness.

Add lemon zest. Beat until fluffy.

Frost top and sides of one layer and sprinkle with flaked coconut. Top with second layer and frost. Sprinkle flaked coconut on top and sides.

This makes a small, rather dense cake. Recipe can be doubled for a grander, four layer cake. Baked as a sheet cake, it looks nice decorated to resemble a US flag, with blueberries for the star field, and raspberries or halved strawberries for the stripes.

—*Tracey Enerson Wood*
St. Petersburg, FL

The Texas Rattler

Over the course of my civilian career, I worked in Sales, Field Engineering, and Product Development. I was able to be on the forefront of many new product developments and played a key role in defining data which was critical to those decisions. My military background, my education, and my life experience prepared me well for the roles to which I was assigned and I dearly loved doing all the unique things that I was exposed to over thirty-five years in that industry.

I am a political conservative who cares deeply for his country, its heritage, constitution, and Rule of Law.

My military service occurred in my younger years of life, when I was a rather picky eater—more or less a meat and potatoes guy. My time in service included travel to all regions of the USA, as well as a number of countries scattered across the globe, which opened my culinary horizons.

I developed a curiosity about food, and took a greater interest in cooking. This is one of my favorite dishes that evolved from that period in my life, and the interest I had gained in Cajun-based cooking. This dish is hearty, appetizing and on the spicy side, which can be adjusted to your own taste buds. I hope you enjoy it as much as I do.

Italian-Sausage Pasta

Serves 8

Ingredients:

1 pkg. Italian sausage links (about 5) (I use either sweet or spicy)

2 large yellow or white onions

1 celery stalk

2–3 tbsp. butter or ½ c. cooking oil

1 lb. bulk ground Italian sausage (I use "spicy")

2 tbsp. fresh or jarred chopped garlic

8 oz. sliced roasted red peppers, drained (I use jarred, Marzetta brand)

2 (15-oz.) cans of red beans, drained (I use the New Orleans Style)

½ pkg. of bow tie pasta or rice

1 (16-oz.) jar of creamy or garlic Alfredo sauce

32 oz. chicken broth

Slap Yo' Mama Cajun Seasoning

Directions:

Place the Italian sausage links on a sheet pan into a 400°F oven and cook until dark on the outside, about 15 minutes.

Chop the onions into coarse pieces of about a quarter inch.

Slice celery stalk into three to four celery sticks, then chop into quarter-inch pieces (be careful with this stuff—it gets bitter if you use too much).

Use a Dutch oven on the stove-top on medium heat. Add a couple tabs of butter or cover bottom in cooking oil. Brown the ground Italian sausage, making sure to break it up as it cooks. I like to use a potato masher here and press the meat as it cooks—it separates nicely using that method.

When the sausage is lightly brown, add onions, celery, and garlic, and stir to sweat them down a bit, then reduce the heat. Add sliced red peppers to the mixture (I like to chop them up a bit prior to adding) then stir.

Don't forget to check on the sausage cooking in the oven and stir the mixture on the stove top.

You may need to turn the stove top down a bit and add some broth or wine to keep from sticking. Add more butter if you like.

Add red beans to the mixture. Stir.

Cook the pasta according to instructions on the package, then drain.

Remove the sausage links from the oven, ensure they are cooked through, cool them a bit, and then slice them into rounds about ⅛-inch thick. Add the sausage rounds to the veggie mix on the stove.

Add the bow tie pasta and stir.

Now add the sauce and stir the mixture well.

Taste the mixture. If you want it spicier, you can add some of the cajun seasoning and salt/pepper to taste.

Note: For variation you can substitute rice for the pasta.

I use an 8 oz. boil-in-the-bag Jasmine White Rice—two bags into a microwave container.

Add broth/water mixture plus some Cajun seasoning.

Cook on high for three 3-minute cycles, remove, and allow the bags to absorb the remaining moisture.

When cooled for handling, empty the bags back into the container and fluff the rice with a fork. You can then add it to the veggie mixture.

—Wayne Brown
Arlington, TX
Cpt., USAF Jan 1971–Jun 1977
Service: C-130E, EC, & H model Navigator/Instructor Navigator in Europe, South America, Central America, Southeast Asia

Food Helps Friendships Last Decades

Johnny Brazilian is a family favorite recipe. It is the kind of recipe that someone always asks for a copy. Our first duty station was Okinawa, Japan, from 1969–1972. Recently, I had a friend who was stationed with us back then send me an email asking for the recipe again. It seems that his copy had been misplaced and he was quite anxious to get another. It's one of their family favorites also.

Johnny Brazilian

Ingredients:

1 lb. seashell pasta
3 lb. lean ground beef
Garlic powder, salt, and pepper to taste
2 tbsp. vegetable oil
2 medium to large onions, chopped
2 medium to large bell peppers, chopped
1 (10–11-oz.) can condensed tomato soup
1 (10–11-oz.) can condensed mushroom
    soup

1 (15-oz.) can whole kernel corn, drained
1 (10–12-oz.) jar of your favorite olives,
    drained and thinly sliced
2 tbsp. Worcestershire sauce
Several drops of Louisiana hot sauce
½ lb. Velveeta cheese

Directions:

Cook pasta according to package directions.

Season ground beef with garlic, salt, and pepper, then brown and drain meat.

Sear onion and peppers in vegetable oil. Add in the cooked ground beef, soups, and drained corn. Let simmer for an hour.

Add olives, Worcestershire sauce, hot sauce, and Velveeta cheese. Continue to simmer until cheese is melted. Serve over pasta.

—Linda Mandell
Wife of Robert W. Mandell, CDR, USN, Ret

Off-Roading in Afghanistan

One of my more memorable meals in Afghanistan came courtesy of a meeting with the commander of an Afghan National Security Forces Kandak (battalion) that was providing local security for some of the key infrastructure in our area of operations. They were located out in a sparse patch of desert about an hour from our base, which required us to drive our busted old pickup truck through at least four or five checkpoints to get there.

Checkpoints were always fun since we often had to rely on our interpreter (*terp*) to build rapport with the poor saps manning the checkpoints so they wouldn't try to search our vehicle, all the while hoping they wouldn't notice our communications gear or the weapons hidden under an Afghan *patu* (shawl) on the floorboard. In the backseat was arguably the most important item in the vehicle—a case of bottled water—needed for last-ditch bribing of any particularly stubborn guards.

I knew it was going to be an interesting day when we spotted one of the Kandak's Toli (company) commanders, who had met us at the turnoff from the main road. He had the grizzled look of a mountain bear and a hand shake like a vice grip, and was driving one of their signature green pickup trucks that vaguely resembled what a "technical" should look like, but in place of a proper machinegun mount over the rear bed there was simply a soldier comically sitting on a plastic lawn chair while resting his weapon over the centerline of the cab.

As we followed them toward their outpost, things got even more interesting once we realized we were now off-roading through the remnants of an old Soviet minefield, complete with little red flags and a couple of Afghan soldiers laden in bulky bomb suits cautiously scanning the sand with metal detectors.

Once we arrived at their outpost, we jumped out to greet the Kandak commander and make introductions. The few Toli commanders present were battle-hardened former *mujahedeen*; they had all been fighting in one form or another since they were teenagers in the 1980s during the Soviet occupation.

The meeting itself lasted a little over an hour, the majority of time spent drinking green tea and chatting. Afterwards, the Kandak commander insisted that we join him and his men for a meal. While they had previously mentioned sitting down for a meal after this meeting, we assumed they were just being polite, and had no expectation or real desire to eat at their remote outpost.

The commander, however, was a stickler for hospitality (as most Afghans are) and insisted we join them, to which our terp strongly advised we should accept as it would be rude to decline. (Unbeknown to our hosts, I had just gotten over a lovely case of the "Afghan shits" about a week prior with the help of some Cipro from our medic, and had no desire to eat anything that might cause that level of intestinal distress again.)

We all shared sideways glances and then agreed to join them, even despite the concern we registered after looking at their makeshift dining facility. It encompassed the remains of a partially demolished brick building, with their cook traversing through the gaping hole in a collapsed wall between the kitchen and the "stove"—a large outdoor bonfire with a huge soot-black pot resting over it. While their cook was obviously a very resourceful individual, "sanitary" is not the first word that came to mind when describing his set-up.

We all sat down at a rickety table with makeshift place settings, mismatched glasses, and pitchers with what I assume was well water, and even more tea. Once we were all seated, the cook began hauling the meal over, which consisted of a huge platter of a signature Afghan dish, Kabuli Pulao, with a heaping of miscellaneous grilled lamb parts unceremoniously dumped on the top. A couple side dishes contained fresh vegetables and what we referred to as bread Frisbees, a naan-like bread in the shape of a giant flat donut. We each gathered a polite-sized portion onto our plates, and hesitantly started to dig in.

Any trepidations I had about the cleanliness of the kitchen gave way when I put the first bite in my mouth. This was not the first time I had eaten Pulao; it's a very common dish across Afghanistan. But something about this particular meal grew on me with every savory-sweet bite of rice and lamb that practically melted in my mouth. In addition to being delicious, there was just something wholly authentic about it.

When I reached the end of my plate, instead of being worried about my stomach, I found myself asking our terp if it would be rude of me to ask for seconds or thirds. He was also excited about the meal, explaining how it reminded him of some of his early days as a child growing up in Afghanistan, before his family was forced to depart for another country.

We left that meeting full and happy, and extremely grateful to our gracious hosts with whom we maintained a strong relationship. The commander and I hit it off from there forward, and he promised to take me to see a game of the Afghan national pastime Buzkashi, where dozens of men on horses fight each other to carry a beheaded goat across a field and drop it near a pole to score points or win wagers (he did follow through on this promise a couple months later—it was some spectacle).

We were all impressed with how that cook was able to make such a fine meal in such austere conditions, and none of us had any inklings of "intestinal distress" afterwards. We made a point of paying them visits every now again throughout the rest of my deployment, and likewise hosted some of them to our dining facility to reciprocate as often as possible.

Based on advice I got from our terps and various locals, this is my best attempt at a recipe for Kabuli Pulao. I've tried to recreate it a few times, and to be frank, just like many things in Afghanistan it's fairly challenging and I've never made it quite as good as I remembered it. If you research it on the Internet, you will find different folks with many different versions of the recipe. I'd suggest that if you can find a local Afghan restaurant nearby, see if you can try it first from an expert before experimenting at home.

Afghan Rice (Kabuli Pulao)

Serves 12–15

Ingredients:

Topping:
¼ c. chopped almonds
¼ c. chopped pistachios
½ cup vegetable oil
1 c. raisins or sultanas
1 c. julienned carrots (the pieces of carrot should be sort of matchstick sized, i.e., not shredded)
1 tbsp. sugar
½ tsp. cardamom powder*

Main Ingredients:
5 c. long grain Basmati rice (soak in water for 1 hour prior to cooking)
Approx. 4–5 pounds of lamb, chicken, or beef
2–3 yellow onions, chopped
4–5 garlic cloves, chopped
½ c. vegetable oil
2 tbsp. *garam masala* spice blend **
1 tsp. salt
3 tbsp. sugar

* You can grind the cardamom freshly from dried pods if you want, but be sure to thoroughly grind the "meat" of the cardamom and remove all of the shells.

** *Garam masala* is a blend of black pepper, cardamom, cinnamon, cloves, coriander, cumin, turmeric, and a few other spices. If you want to be more authentic about it, you can buy each of those individual spices and grind them up. I'd suggest just buying the garam masala for the sake of simplicity.

Directions:

Meat and Stock Preparation:

Whichever meat you choose, remove meat from bone or buy boneless, and cut meat into large chunks about three to four inches in size. If using a whole chicken, you can opt to portion it and cook with bones in.

Heat ½ cup of vegetable oil in a large pot, add chopped onions, and fry until they are well browned but not burnt.

Add meat, chopped garlic, 1 tablespoon garam masala, and 1 teaspoon salt. Mix ingredients and spread the meat across the bottom area of the pot so that it will brown. Cook for a few minutes, then flip meat to brown the other side.

Once you are comfortable with the level of browning on the meat, add 5–6 cups of water and another tablespoon of garam masala.

Reduce to low heat, and cook for about an hour, or until the meat is tender and the stock has reduced by about half. Make sure to also scrape up any crust on the bottom of the pot to ensure it will marry with the stock.

Topping Preparation (do this while waiting for your meat stock to reduce):

Heat up a frying pan and gently toast the ¼ cup almonds and ¼ cup pistachios until they brown a little. Put them off to the side.

Add ½ cup vegetable oil into the frying pan and add raisins. Cook for only 1–2 minutes until the raisins plump up, then add the carrots and mix in a tablespoon of sugar to help caramelize the carrots. Cook for about 5 minutes then add in the nuts and cardamom powder. Mix everything, then remove from the oil and set it off to the side for later.

Save the oil in the skillet as you can re-use it for both re-browning the meat and starting the caramelized sugar which you will add to the rice.

Rice Preparation (do this while waiting for your meat stock to reduce):

Ensure your rice was soaked in water for 1 hour prior to starting (but don't oversoak, as that can make the rice too soft).

Bring a large pot full of water to a boil.

Add the 5 cups rice and salt to flavor. Cook for about 5–10 minutes or until the rice is approximately two-thirds of the way cooked.

It should be soft on the outside, but still a little crunchy in the middle, sort of rice al dente.

You will need to remove some rice every few minutes and test it.

Once the rice is ready, strain it, and then put it back into a large oven-proof pot (with a lid), and set this off to the side.

Final Preparation:

Once your meat stock has finished cooking, remove the pieces of meat and if needed, re-brown them with the oil in the skillet you used to make the toppings (add a little more oil if needed).

Set the meat off to the side. (If you were cooking with bone-in meat, you can opt to remove the bones at this stage).

In the same oil, add 3 tablespoons of sugar and heat for a few minutes until the sugar has caramelized to a brown colored syrup. Pour this mixture over the rice in the large pot, then also add about 2 cups of the meat stock over the rice.

Mix the rice and liquid until the rice turns a nice brown color. Ensure there is enough stock in the rice that it is a little bit wet, we will need this moisture to create steam that will further cook and saturate the rice, meat, and toppings. Add pinches of salt, cardamom, and garam masala to the rice if needed.

Once you are satisfied with the rice, place your pieces of meat on top of the rice to one side, and place the toppings on top of the rice to the other side.

Poke a few holes in the rice with the handle of a wooden spoon down to the bottom of the pot, this creates channels for the steam. Cover the pot with a well-fitting lid, and cook in the oven on low heat (about 250F) for 30 minutes (this step can also be done on low heat over the stovetop if needed).

To plate, remove the pieces of meat and toppings. Layer about half of the rice on your serving dish, then the meat, then the rest of the rice over the meat. Finally, layer the toppings over the surface of the rice.

—*Scott Riffle*
US Navy

Photo by Kristen Riffle

PART VI: COMFORT FOODS
What Gets us Through the Difficult Times

Pie Lady

Instead of a diamond engagement ring, my father presented my mother with a sturdy piece of off-white American Tourister luggage. He was in the Navy, a Sea Bee, an Indiana farm boy who dreamed of the ocean and wanted nothing more than to see the world. She was the ninth child and sixth daughter of Italian American immigrants, living in a busy, noisy household bursting with relatives, food, and shrines to saints and the Virgin Mary. My mother had no desire to go anywhere at all. She loved her small mill town; she loved her small state. But when my father gave her that suitcase, he told her she was going to see the world, with him.

For their honeymoon they drove 860 miles in an early winter blizzard so that she could meet his relatives in Greensburg, Indiana. To his family, my father was special. He'd left home at seventeen to join the Navy, lived in San Francisco where he had a brief engagement to a Nob Hill debutante, then was shipped off to China to fight communism. They didn't know the stories that we later heard, how starving people dropped dead right in the street and they were ordered not to help them or they'd have to pay for the funeral. He saw opium dens and brothels and shootouts.

His brothers and sisters thought my mother the most exotic bird: dark curly hair, olive skin, a Roman nose, a Catholic who wouldn't eat meat on Friday. Their food—chicken fried in lard, beans and soups with ham hocks, copious amounts of beer—turned her stomach. At nineteen years old, she'd never eaten food at someone's house who wasn't Italian, and she was frightened and disgusted and only wanted to go home. When she offered to make spaghetti and meatballs for everyone, she couldn't even find garlic in the grocery store. And to my father, *home* was an elusive place, somewhere to stop for gossip and home cooked meals on your way to other places.

When they first met, my mother not only fell in love with my father; she fell in love with a tall, blond, blue-eyed sailor in a white dress uniform. She didn't think about how sailors went off to sea, often for long periods of time. She didn't think about how he wouldn't be based in Newport forever, or even for very long. There was always the next base somewhere else, a fact that excited my wanderlust dad and made my mother sad and weary.

He was at sea when their first child was born. My mother, just turned twenty, married less than a year, found herself alone in a Navy hospital, giving birth. She still describes that as one of her lowest points in her life—scared and ignorant of the ways women gave birth and my father so far away. Still, she named my brother after my father, happily adding Junior at the end of his name, then promptly nicknamed him Skip, short for Skipper, a nod to my Navy father.

After he returned, Skip already six months old, my father's next post was in Naples, Italy. He thought this would please my mother—her family had come from a small town near Naples fifty years earlier, and many of them still talked with great nostalgia about the old country. But Naples was across a very big ocean from her mother and her sisters, and my mother didn't want to go. So my father went alone. He secured an apartment in the upscale Vamero neighborhood, and wrote love letters telling my mother how he couldn't live without her.

Ultimately she relented, reluctantly. Six months after he left, my father flew home to get her. Surely a part of him worried that if he wasn't there, she might not get on that plane to Naples. The day he arrived, her favorite sister went into the hospital for a routine wisdom tooth extraction. Mom brought her some magazines and promised to go back later, but after six months apart, my young parents ended up losing themselves in a night of romance. The next morning, the hospital called: her sister had died from an allergic reaction to the anesthesia.

In overwhelming grief, my mother went through with the move to Naples. But not until after the funeral. My father flew back alone, and a few weeks later my mother left her bereft mother, her sister's widowed husband and two motherless children, and boarded the Navy plane with my year-old brother in her arms. She'd never flown before, and everything about it terrified her. The plane made frequent unexplained stops, and my mother cried the whole way—over losing her favorite sister, over being alone so far from home, over this move itself.

But something happened in Naples. To her surprise, she loved hearing her native tongue spoken, loved the laundry hung across clothesline suspended across buildings, loved how my brother charmed the vegetable man and the baker and the sausage maker. She taught herself to cook there—ruining pots of beans and overcooking pasta and undercooking meats. But by the time they left three years later, she was a Navy wife, ready to go wherever their next post sent them.

Although she was always homesick, by the time I came along a year later, my mother was able to pack up our belongings, set up our furniture in new homes, shop the PX, and get us enrolled in school with ease. To me, she was one of the most competent people I knew. And part of that competence came in the form of what she perfected during those Navy years: pies. Beautiful pies. Back at home, her own mother made pies from the fruit she grew in the yard: blueberries, cherries, apples. But my mother's pies were modern, things of beauty. Chocolate cream and lemon meringue. She never made one without the other, and she brought one of each to the pot lucks and celebrations the Navy families always seemed to be having.

My father's pals and their wives loved my mother's Italian cooking, the meatballs and eggplant parmesan and veal scaloppini. But it was pie that my mother insisted on making. Looking back, I see now that those pies—so American, so contemporary—represented her own independence, her growing up and away from that big Italian family. Not that she ever stopped missing home, or yearning to return, but rather that out there in the big world my father had promised to show her, she was her own woman.

The lemon meringue remains my favorite, and I have had many lemon meringue pies in my life. Pies made with higher, sweeter meringues. Pies made with real lemon curd. But I have never had one as good as my mother's. Her topping does not soar, but is white and sugary and topped with small browned peaks (that even now I steal off the top when I pass one of her pies). Her lemon filling is made from a mix. Her crust is store bought.

No matter. One taste and I am back in our apartment in Arlington, Virginia, my father at work for Admiral Rickover at the Pentagon. The door opens and he is there in his uniform, and my mother's face lights up as she runs to him and lets him take her into his arms for a movie star kiss. My brother is eating the chocolate cream pie, I am eating the lemon meringue, and it is so sweet, so sweet, that pie, this transient life we have together, this family.

Gogo's Lemon Meringue Pie

Serves 8

Ingredients:

1 store bought pie crust (preferably Pillsbury)

1 Box Jell-O Lemon Pudding and Pie Filling, not instant

2 egg yolks

½ c. sugar

4 egg whites

4 tbsp. powdered sugar, plus more for sprinkling

1 tsp. corn starch

A few drops lemon juice

Directions:

Preheat oven to 350°F. Bake pie crust until lightly browned, about 10–12 minutes.

Make lemon filling according to package directions. You will need the egg yolks, sugar, and water. Add to browned pie crust.

As it cools, make meringue:

Add remaining ingredients in a bowl and beat with electric mixer until stiff peaks form.

Sprinkle cooled lemon filling evenly with powdered sugar.

Gently pour meringue onto pie and bake for three minutes, or until peaks have lightly browned.

—Ann Hood
Bestselling author of
The Book That Matters Most
www.annhood.us

Dark Time

It was dark, but it would get much darker for all Americans and the world. Inside our very small apartment on the third floor of a German family's home, the Armed Forces Radio station was playing softly in the background. I probably had it on for some music. At the age of twenty-one, I had married Rich in June and we had moved from New York City to Heilbronn Am Neckar, West Germany.

At twenty-two years old, Rich had graduated with a BSME from CCNY and a two-year commitment to the Army through ROTC. Before we married and moved, he had been working at Pratt and Whitney in Connecticut, and I as a RN in the recovery room at Sloan Kettering Cancer Memorial in Manhattan.

Now it was late November 1963, eighteen years after World War II ended, and in the middle of the Cold War. It was our first time out of the country. The Berlin Wall had gone up two years before and the Cuban crisis had occurred a year earlier. President Kennedy had sent a few Green Berets into Vietnam.

It was cold and dark outside but inside was filled with laughter and light. Rich, as a new lieutenant, was away at the kasern. He and the company's other officers were meeting with the German mayor and officials of the town, in an outreach to enhance relationships between the two groups.

Years earlier, my sister had been working on her Girl Scout pen pal badge and was paired with Brigitte, a pen pal in Heilbronn Am Neckar . . . of all places. I had a ready-made friend. Her family and friends became mine. So it was, that night after dinner, Brigitte and her friend were helping me, a new bride, to master some German dishes. At some point we realized the music had stopped and an urgent voice was speaking. We stopped everything, hearing only the unthinkable words . . . President Kennedy was dead. Assassinated! Assassinated? Who was the last President assassinated? What happened afterwards? Would I have to travel across Europe to get back home?

Brigitte and her friend left. I was stunned, confused, and anxious. We did not have a phone. Our non-English speaking landlord and family did not have a phone. I did not have a car, as Rich used ours to go to work. I walked everywhere in the daytime, including to the Heilbronn base, but now it was very dark. We did not have money except for daily needs. I was taking lessons in German, but was still at an infantile level.

I assumed we were going to be at war. It must have been the Russians. Would the Russians invade from East Germany? Rich would not come home, I knew because I had experienced the exercises, "going into the field." In fact it happened the first night I had arrived from The States. We were in bed and heard the pebbles thrown at our window (because we did not have a phone) and off he went. I did not know when he would return. Some exercises lasted months, I had been told; luckily that time he was back the next day.

This was different—this was the real thing. How would I get home to the States?

I did not know if I would see Rich again. I felt so alone and my cold hands stayed glued to the radio, which was the only option to quench my thirst for knowledge.

I planned to walk to the base the next morning and find out what would happen. At an earlier time during an informational session for wives, I was informed in case of a forced evacuation I would be one of the last to go because Rich was in for two years and we lived *on the Economy* (not in government housing). This was not comforting.

Rich returned the next day. It had not been the Russians but an unbalanced individual, Lee Harvey Oswald. My husband told me his story: the group had finished dinner and were at the bowling alley. Suddenly the mayor walked to the center of the lanes and spoke to his German countrymen in rapid German as he rolled down his white shirt sleeves. He then turned to the Americans and said, "I think you want to be alone at this time."

The company went into action out into the field. Rich's platoon made liquid oxygen for the Redstone missiles, the first missile to carry a live nuclear warhead. The missiles were aimed toward Russia. No war this time.

Sauerbraten

An easy meal that you can adjust to your own tastes and desires as to how much time you want to spend with the preparation or what is on sale.

Serves 8

Ingredients:

4–6 lb. of rump, bottom, or top round roast, or boneless chuck

2 c. boiling red wine vinegar

2 c. boiling water (or beef broth)

1 good-sized onion, thickly sliced

4 bay leaves

6 whole cloves

10 whole peppercorns

1 tbsp. salt

1 tbsp. sugar

3 tbsp. vegetable oil

12 gingersnap cookies, crushed finely (use rolling pin to crush cookies in a Ziploc plastic bag)

Directions:

Place beef in a ceramic or non-reactive metal bowl.

Boil together all ingredients, combining everything from the red wine vinegar through 1 tablespoon sugar.

Pour boiling liquid to cover or almost cover the beef. Cover with lid or wrap.

Place the covered bowl in a refrigerator for 3 days, turning once or twice daily. You can get away with 2 days but I have found the marinade does a better job in 3 days.

Remove meat from the marinade. Pat the meat dry.

Heat vegetable oil using a large Dutch oven and brown all sides of the meat, about 8–12 minutes. (As an alternative, I have skipped this step and just removed the meat from the marinade and placed it in a crock pot.)

In either case, pour the marinade over the meat and cover. If you use the Dutch oven, turn heat to medium/low. In a crock pot, turn on high. Simmer until meat is tender, approximately 3½–4 hours.

Remove the meat to a carving board or platter and let stand while you strain the liquid of all spices. Discard the spices.

Return marinade to the cooking pot.

Add crushed gingersnap cookies to the simmering liquid, stirring this gravy over medium heat until thickened, perhaps 8–10 min.

Slice the sauerbraten.

Serve with the gingersnap gravy, spätzle, buttered sliced steamed cabbage with caraway seeds, or red pickled cabbage.

Apple strudel is a good ending to the meal.

Enjoy.

—Joan Lander
St. Petersburg, FL

A New World to Discover

There are some, like me, who are pretty good cooks, if given a basic recipe and quality ingredients to work with. I have enough experience to make quite a few things with no recipe at all or modify one to suit our tastes, and only measure ingredients when baking. There are those who need step-by-step guidelines and actually measure that ⅛ teaspoon of ground pepper.

A whole other class is the natural cooks. People like my son, who thinks up flavor combinations that I would never

Artwork by Carol Van Drie. *Photos by Steve Dean Photography.*

dream of, and they're amazing. And my dear friend and out-law, Carol Van Drie, who packs more flavor into a dish than seems humanly possible. I still remember the first taste of her tortellini soup, the hearty richness of the sausage, the fully developed tomato, the creamy counterpoint and slight chewiness of the tortellini. Fresh herbs dancing to the top of the flavor profile, and a finish of aged Parmesan. Heaven.

Over many years, and many, many military moves, we shared our love of food. Pasta Faggioli in New York State, along with the world's best pizza. We cooked. We ate. We laughed. We bonded over grouper in Florida. Shared potty training horror stories over fajitas in California, enjoyed street schnitzel from a *Schnell Imbiss* in Germany. Carol could taste something once, then re-create it, usually improving it as well.

Now both of our husbands are retired from the military, and we are empty nesters. There are no longer five (combined) children to feed three meals and multiple snacks each day. Middle-age brings with it a need to watch calories and other dietary restrictions. We are happy to hand the cooking reins over to our now adult children and their spouses, while we spoil the grandchildren. So although we still bond over food, cooking no longer occupies a large chunk of our days.

Carol found a new world open up to her in May 2013. Due to foot surgery, her doctor ordered three months of bed rest, and she frantically searched for something to do besides read email and watch television. She accidently stumbled on the fascinating world of needle-felting.

"I see everything now with an eye toward interpreting it onto a felted canvas, with various textures and colors of wool. This ability is a God-given gift, as I have no formal training in the arts," Carol tells her many fans.

But Carol is using her innate sense of beauty and balance to create her art, the same skills that made her cooking special. Indeed, her art is rich and colorful, full of love and warmth, just like a bowl of her tortellini soup.

—*Tracey Enerson Wood*
St. Petersburg, FL

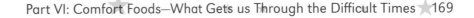

A Family Favorite

This was the "on demand" comfort food my husband requested upon returning from many Army deployments. When my son came back from his deployment to Afghanistan, it was the first meal he requested of his new wife, asking her to "get the recipe from Mom."

My family also asks for this soup for any special occasion. I have served this to beloved family, friends, and neighbors in Europe and the US for years, and have had repeated requests for the recipe. I'm guessing there are a number of Army wives who have made one form of this recipe or another after sharing it with so many others during my husband's thirty-one-year Army career.

When I prepare it or eat it, the aroma and taste instantly bring to mind wonderful memories of our service to this great country.

Photo by G. Szenas & D.L. Phelps

Italian Sausage and Tortellini Soup

Serves 12

Ingredients:

1 lb. sweet Italian sausage, bulk or casings removed

¼ c. olive oil, or less, as needed

1 c. coarsely chopped onions

2 cloves garlic, chopped/sliced

5 c. beef broth

1 c. Burgundy wine

16-oz. can chopped Italian flavored tomatoes, undrained

8-oz. can tomato sauce

¼ c. chopped fresh basil

¼ c. fresh oregano

1½ c. zucchini, thickly sliced, then cut crossways

1 c. thinly sliced carrots

¼ c. chopped fresh parsley

1 medium green pepper, coarsely chopped

Sea salt to taste

1 tbsp. ground black pepper

1 medium yellow pepper, coarsely chopped

10 oz. meat or cheese filled tortellini or small ravioli

Fresh shredded Parmesan cheese

Directions:

Brown sausage in a large frying pan. If too dry, add a little olive oil. Once browned, remove sausage and drain, but reserve about 1 tablespoon of the drippings. Sauté onions and garlic in reserved drippings until tender.

Place sautéed sausage, onion, and garlic in a Dutch oven. Add broth, wine, tomatoes, tomato sauce, basil, oregano. Bring to a boil and add salt and pepper to taste. Reduce heat and simmer uncovered for 30 minutes.

Skim fat from soup. Then stir in zucchini, carrots, parsley, and green and yellow pepper. Simmer covered an additional 35–45 minutes. If liquid is diminished, add more broth and/or wine.

Add tortellini, cover, and bring to a boil again. When tortellini are desired tenderness, about another 10–15 minutes, remove from heat.

Serve with Parmesan cheese to sprinkle on top and crusty Italian bread.

Tips: Do not over-salt—depending on the type of broth, no additional salt may be required.

To save time and clean up, you can sauté the sausage, onion, and garlic in the Dutch oven, then drain the fat before adding the remaining ingredients.

To bring it to an Italian, flavorful richness, add more olive oil to taste.

—*Carol Van Drie*
Okemos, MI

Reality Arrives in a Little Brown Bag

Food is a funny thing in the military. It can be the one normal thing in life that's relatable to everyone, regardless of whether they're in the military. For me, I can remember being in Ranger School's last phase in Florida. At that point, you are a different person both physically and mentally. Your body is exhausted but you are mentally tougher than you have ever been. You're kept sequestered from the outside world with the exception of mail and two eight-hour breaks between the three phases.

In Florida, in my MRE (Meals, Ready to Eat), I got a little bag of M&Ms and remember feeling like the candy pulled me back into the reality of what my life was like before Ranger School. Some of the best moments in your life revolve around food and they don't have be complicated or expensive to be memorable. Not every meal is Thanksgiving, but some are just as rewarding.

—Timothy Koester
Former CPT and Ranger, US Army

Crunch-Top Apple Pie

(Not complicated or expensive, but memorable!)

Serves 8

Ingredients:

6 medium tart apples, cored
    and thinly sliced
Unbaked 10-inch pie crust
1 c. granulated sugar
1 c. graham cracker crumbs
½ c. flour
½ c. pecans, chopped
½ tsp. cinnamon
½ c. butter, melted

Photo by G. Szenas and D.L. Phelps

Directions:

Preheat oven to 350°F.

Arrange apples in pastry shell. It will form a heap.

Mix sugar, cracker crumbs, flour, nuts, and cinnamon; sprinkle over apples. Pour butter evenly over topping.

Bake until apples are tender when pierced, about 1 hour.

Serve warm or at room temperature, garnished with whipped cream or ice cream if desired.

—Tracey Enerson Wood,
Adapted from recipe of
Glenice Gile
Wife of US Army Veteran

The Terrifying Cook

My mother, First Lieutenant Genevieve R. (née Biferie) Ward, was an Army nurse and proud graduate of one of the Army's first, post-World War II courses in psychiatric medicine. She was also a terrifying cook. She once imploded a turkey—in an autoclave no less. And we won't talk about her Nagasaki Ribs. No, seriously, we won't talk about them. The National Security Agency determined what she did to the pork on that occasion constituted a weapon of mass destruction and classified the details.

For years, my father, a career Medical Service Corps officer, dragged us to the base hospital mess hall for every holiday meal *not* prepared by the relatives or sympathetic friends. At the time, he claimed it was a matter of building morale and troop cohesion. Many years later, he confessed, "It was the only way I could be sure we'd get a decent dinner. Your mother is a wonderful woman. But she's not a very good cook."

Talk about the understatement of two centuries. Mother's cooking was a byword in the Army—and not nice one, either. Commanders' wives (it was always wives back then) developed special party protocols to navigate Mom's events. First the CO's wife would drag me out of my room, and demand I identify the perpetrator—er, preparer of each dish on the buffet table. Then she would carefully push the offending matter to the rim of the relevant serving plates, and pass the word along the spousal chain of command which dishes to avoid. I understand the "Genevieve Protocol," as it came to be called, reduced post-cocktail party hospitalizations for food poisoning by 80 percent Army-wide.

Genevieve R. B. Ward, Women's Army Corps., WWII.

But there was one dish—one dish she never served to Dad's fellow officers or their spouses—one dish at which she was without peer. Mom's spaghetti sauce could reduce gourmets to tears of rapture and cause angels to drool into their horns. Built Southern Italian-style from a base of oil and garlic, it took forever to make, but it went with everything from meatballs to softshell crabs. It was our panacea for Dad's work woes, my growing pains, and temporary quarters in a sixth-floor walk-up with no curtains or blinds for the windows. It was the dish we shared with family and true friends, and the celebration meal that signaled my recovery from every childhood illness. It was love in a pot, and to this day I can't make it without feeling her warm hand over mine as I stir the sauce and set the pasta on the boil.

What's a little ptomaine turkey or death-dealing ribs compared to that?

John and Genevieve Ward on honeymoon, 1947.

Genevieve Ward's Spaghetti Sauce and Tender Meatballs

Serves 12

Ingredients:

Olive oil

2 heaping tablespoons minced garlic (can be pre-roasted)

10 c. tomatoes, peeled, cored, and lightly mashed

(About 10–15 pounds fresh tomatoes; if you use canned, make sure the can contains nothing but tomatoes—or tomatoes and basil—no tomato paste)

½ c. parsley leaves (preferably Italian parsley), minced

1 c. fresh basil leaves, minced

½ tbsp. fresh oregano, or ½ tsp. dried oregano (optional)

½ c. grated Romano or Parmesan cheese, or a combination of both

Ground black pepper to taste

Red pepper flakes to taste

Peeled carrot (optional)

Directions:

In a large stainless steel, aluminum, or porcelain-lined saucepan, sauté the garlic in olive oil over high heat until golden. (Do not allow to burn.)

Add tomatoes, herbs, about 1 teaspoon fresh ground black pepper, and ½ teaspoon crushed red pepper flakes. Reduce heat to medium.

Sift the cheese about one tablespoon at a time into the tomatoes, stirring after each addition so the cheese does not clump and melt before it's mixed into the tomatoes. Bring to a low boil, stirring frequently. Reduce heat to low and simmer uncovered, stirring every 10–15 minutes, for two hours.

After two hours, the sauce should be reduced by roughly 25 percent. If it appears to be reducing too fast, add more water. Taste. Add additional cheese, pepper, or basil if desired. (Do not salt, especially if you use canned tomatoes. If you like a saltier sauce, add more cheese.)

If you prefer a smoother sauce, cool the sauce and mash the tomatoes. Resume cooking until sauce reaches the desired consistency.

If the tomatoes aren't as sweet as you'd like or too much parsley left the sauce a little bitter, add a carrot to absorb the bitterness, but remove before mashing or serving.

Tender Meatballs

Ingredients:

½ c. fresh basil leaves, finely chopped
½ c. fresh parsley leaves, finely chopped
1½ lb. lean ground beef or ground venison
1½ lb. sweet Italian sausage
½ c. grated Parmesan or Romano, or a combination of both
½ c. plain bread crumbs
½ tsp. ground black pepper
½ tsp. red pepper flakes
½ tbsp. fresh oregano, or ½ tsp. dried oregano (optional)
½–1 c. cooled spaghetti sauce

Directions:

Preheat oven to 350°F.

Combine all ingredients except spaghetti sauce.

Add enough spaghetti sauce to make the meat mixture easy to shape into balls 1–1¼ inch in diameter. Any extra sauce can be returned to the sauce pot.

Place balls on a rack in a low roasting pan. (It doesn't matter if they touch.) Brown 12–15 minutes. Turn over and brown another 12–15 minutes.

Add meatballs to sauce. (Discard the fat and juices in the roasting pan or save for another recipe.) Simmer another 30–45 minutes.

—Jean Marie Ward
Daughter of COL (Ret.) John J. Ward, US Army
and Genevieve R. Biferie, former 1LT, US Army

A Toast to Normandy

My father, Bob Enerson, was a soldier and survivor of the invasion of Normandy, France, in June, 1944. He told the story of when the Americans pushed the occupying Germans back from the Normandy beaches and coast, the local French farmers and village people would greet and celebrate their arrivals. They would come out cheering, offering open bottles of Calvados brandy and pouring drinks for the GI's.

Calvados is a brandy made from the locally grown apples by the farmers of the Normandy region. The farmers often told the GI's stories of how the Germans would invade their homes in search of it. The Frenchmen were proud of how it survived, carefully hidden in their cellars.

It was a custom for many years for the surviving GI's to have a drink and toast of Calvados on the anniversary of D-Day.

Calvados Brandy is widely available in the US today.

Robert Enerson Sr. (on right) with unidentified friends in France, 1944.

Calvados Bread Pudding

Serves 6

Ingredients:
3 c. bread cubess (4 slices)
4 eggs
2 c. milk
½ c. brown sugar
2 tsp. vanilla extract
2 tsp. cinnamon
½ tsp. nutmeg
½ tsp. salt
½ c. golden raisins
Topping: ½ c. Calvados brandy

Directions:

Preheat oven to 350°F. Mix all the ingredients except brandy, and transfer to a baking dish. Bake for 45 minutes. Pour the Calvados over the bread pudding before serving.

—Robert Enerson Jr.
Richmond, VA

Don't it Make your Blond Hair Brown?

Calvados bread pudding was always served with coffee. Bob Enerson was affectionately nicknamed "Whitey" by his family and friends because of his snow-white hair. Upon his return home at the end of the war, his mother was aghast when she first laid eyes on her son. His hair was now a deep brown, almost black.

"Whitey, what happened to your hair!?" were the first words from her mouth.

His reply, "Ma, it was the Army coffee."

—Christina Enerson
Fairbanks, AK

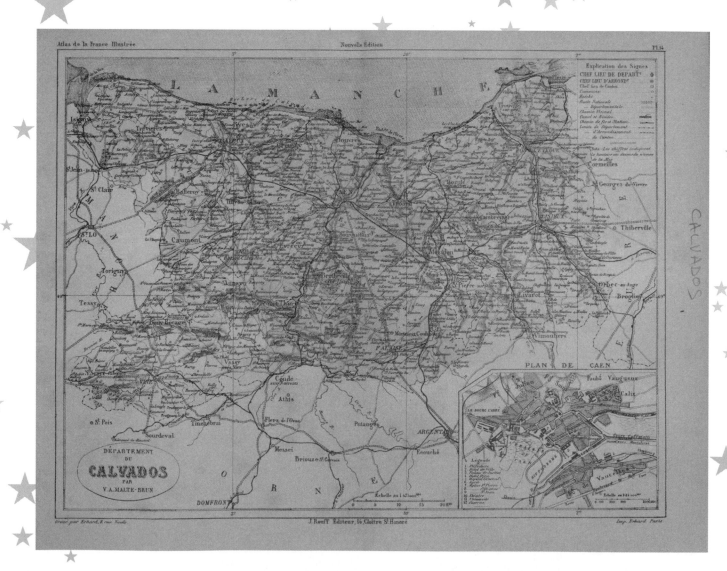

Love and Lasagna

Lasagna is a somewhat time-consuming dish to prepare, but it is one of my husband's favorites. So I call this my "I love you" dish. It is one of his first requests when coming home from the field or from deployment. I like adding roasted vegetables for extra flavor and to make it a healthier dish. Our kids love it too! One benefit of the long cooking time is that I can prepare the dish while my kids are napping. Then once it is in the oven, I can play with them outside for an hour.

When I make lasagna, I often make a double batch: one to eat, one for the freezer. The freezer meal I save for any military family that might need it next. It is my favorite dish to bring to a new mom, when she brings her baby home from the hospital. I have served it to moms and children who visit while our husbands are training in the field. Lasagna makes a great welcoming dish for a new neighbor. I have also brought my lasagna to families suffering unexpected medical problems or emergencies.

The military spouse community is very tight-knit and supportive during trying times. Sometimes, the best way to support someone struggling with bad news is to bring them some hearty food. This lasagna is a healthy and heart-warming comfort dish!

Meat Lasagna with Roasted Vegetables

Makes one 9x13 pan of lasagna, about 8 servings

Ingredients:

2 small zucchini

8 white button mushrooms

Non-stick oil spray

Salt

9 uncooked lasagna noodles (½ a box)

1 lb. ground Italian sausage, mild or hot

1 white onion, chopped

2 cloves garlic, minced

8 leaves fresh basil, chopped

2 (24-oz.) jars pasta sauce, any flavor

16 oz. ricotta cheese (use light, if desired)

2 eggs

½ c. grated Parmesan cheese

4 c. mozzarella cheese, shredded, divided (reduced fat, if desired)

Directions:

Preheat oven to 400°F.

Slice zucchini into thick round slabs, and quarter the mushrooms.

Spray a cooking sheet with non-stick spray, then spread out vegetables in a single layer. Spray them with more non-stick spray, and sprinkle with ¼ teaspoon salt.

Roast in oven for 15 minutes, until tender. When cooled, remove from the baking sheet and chop the vegetables smaller.

Reduce oven heat to 350°F.

Cook lasagna noodles in boiling water, according to package directions. Drain and lay out on paper towels.

Cook sausage in a large frying pan over medium-high heat, breaking into crumbles with the back of a wooden spoon. Add onion and garlic. Once softened and lightly browned, add basil leaves. Stir in 1 jar of pasta sauce. Add the chopped roasted vegetables. Remove from heat.

In a medium bowl, stir together ricotta cheese, eggs, Parmesan cheese, and 2 cups of mozzarella cheese. Save the rest of the cheese for topping.

Spray a 9x13 pan or lasagna pan with nonstick spray.

Place a few tablespoons of pasta sauce from the second jar on the bottom of the dish, and spread into a thin layer. Lay 3 cooked lasagna noodles side by side to form a layer. Top with all of the meat/vegetable/sauce mixture from the frying pan. Top those with 3 more lasagna noodles. Spread all of the cheese/egg mixture into an even layer. Top with 3 more lasagna noodles. Spread the rest of the jar of pasta sauce over the top of the lasagna, covering any noodle edges. Top with the remaining 2 cups of mozzarella cheese.

Cover the pan with aluminum foil. You can now either cook it or freeze it for later. If frozen, defrost in fridge overnight before cooking.

Bake covered at 350°F for 45 minutes. Then remove foil, and bake for 10 more minutes until cheese is melted. Allow to cool slightly before serving.

Author's note: *If time allows, we recommend lightly sautéing the garlic and onion and simmer with sauce, meat, and seasonings on low heat for an hour or two. Also tested with the addition of 1 tablespoon dried Italian seasoning to the sauce and 2 teaspoons in the cheese mixture.*

—Lizann Lightfoot
Author of The Seasoned Spouse blog: www.SeasonedSpouse.com

Photo by Steve Dean Photography

Food and Family Tradition

I come from a very large Italian-American family. My Grandfather was quite the adventurer. He left Calabria, Italy, at the age of fifteen to come to America. He got a job working on the American railways, hammering his way out to the West Coast. He missed home, moved back to Italy, got married, and became a mailman. He joined the Italian Army during WW1.

After the war ended, my grandfather left my grandmother in Italy with four children and moved to America with the hope of giving his family a better way of life. He bought land on Long Island, set up a farm, and grew vegetables and fruit to sell out of the back of his truck.

After more than six years, he had enough money to bring them all over to America and join him. They had two more children but unfortunately, he died from a heart attack at the age of forty-two while my grandmother was pregnant with my dad.

The government tried to take away the children from my grandmother. But this 4'10" woman who spoke only Italian and was fiercely protective, used her broom to chase them away!

Fortunately, they had a huge Italian contingent to help support them. My father grew up poor but surrounded by love and always hopeful for the future. As a teenager, my dad became the sole provider for his mother because all his siblings were married with families of their own.

While working at a deli, he also put himself through college and became an engineer at Grumman Aerospace and eventually, helped put a man on the moon. He was drafted into the Army during the Korean Conflict. Because he had a degree, he taught mathematics to the troops at Aberdeen Proving Grounds in Maryland. It was no surprise that I also became a math teacher!

Flash forward to my childhood: My parents and all my relatives took turns hosting huge family gatherings filled with an abundance of delicious food and lots of laughter. All of my uncles and my father's male cousins were veterans of either WWII (The Big One) or the Korean Conflict.

As a young girl in the 1960s, I was privy to their many stories, both humorous and sad. Through their cigar smoke, I listened to them reminisce about their wartime adventures as well as the stories about the many men they knew and lost. They were very proud men and I know those years overseas, both in Europe and in Asia, helped define who they became.

They also had many differing opinions about the Vietnam Conflict. This helped shape my love of history and my opinions of the military and of war. But most significantly, it taught me the importance of family and how to respect everyone's opinion, whether you agree with them or not. They all thought it was ironic that their pacifist niece who was educating poor kids in the Watts section of Los Angeles married an Army officer!

I have chosen three of my favorite recipes that remind me of family gatherings that as a child gave me both comfort and love.

Beef Brisket

Serves 8

Ingredients:
12 oz. bottled chili sauce
12 oz. ginger ale
1 envelope dry onion soup mix
1 beef brisket

Directions:

Mix first three ingredients and pour over the brisket. May refrigerate for a few hours, or bake immediately.

Bake at 350°F: 2½ hours covered, then 1½ hours uncovered.

Remoulade Sauce

Makes about 2 Cups

Ingredients:

1½ c. mayonnaise

4 green onions, sliced

3 tbsp. chopped parsley

3 tbsp. Creole mustard

1½ tbsp. lemon juice

1 garlic clove, minced

1½ tsp. horseradish

1 tsp. paprika

Directions:

Stir all ingredients together and chill in the refrigerator overnight.

Serve with shrimp or use as a spread on sandwiches.

Hazelnut Semifreddo

Serves 12

Ingredients:

1 c. shelled hazelnuts, prepared as follows:

In a preheated 350°F oven, roast the hazelnuts for 10 minutes, turn them, and roast for 10 more minutes. Let them cool for 10 minutes and remove their skins with a towel. Pulse them in a food processor until coarsely chopped.

13-oz.jar of Nutella
½ c. whole milk
2 tbsp. hazelnut liqueur
½ tsp. vanilla extract
½ tsp. salt
2 c. heavy cream

Directions:

Line 12 muffin pan cups with aluminum foil liners.

Blend Nutella, milk, liqueur, vanilla extract, and salt in a food processor until smooth. Add ¾ cup of hazelnuts and pulse.

Scoop the mixture into a large bowl.

Softly whip heavy cream and fold it into the mixture in the large bowl.

Fill each muffin pan cup and sprinkle with remaining hazelnuts. Freeze the pans for 3 hours.

Remove the semifreddos from the pans, but keep them in their liners. Put them in a freezer bag and freeze them overnight.

To serve, remove the liner, place on a plate, and garnish with chocolate sauce and raspberries or over your favorite pie.

Soup Bone Miracle

Three delicate, charm-like objects nestle in my palm. Carved from a soup bone, each is no more than an inch in length, paper thin with a yellowish tint, and buffed smooth as ivory. Each charm of great significance to the life of a young Union soldier.

Twenty-year-old Friedrich (Fritz) Von Schluembach wrote this note to his wife just before entering the Civil War:

My Beloved Wife, Coelestine, As a sign of my sincere love.

Only pure true love should keep us together and we will go through life happy. There will be storms, robust hard storms, but you will always find love in the storms. Fritz S.

Friedrich joined the New York Volunteer Brigade only to be severely wounded at the Battle of Richmond on June 26, 1862. Captured by the Confederates, he was cast into one of the most brutal prison camps of the Civil War: Libby Prison in Richmond, Virginia.

Prisoners slept on wood floors, no beds or blankets. Thousands lay side by side, wounded, sick, and starving. Meals were sparse, consisting of corn bread or sweet potatoes, and often soldiers received nothing for days.

On one rare occasion, Von Schluembach received a meager bowl of soup. Spotting a small bone floating in the broth, he secretly retrieved the morsel. He began carving the soup bone, a daily ritual, warding off depression, affording hope.

Looking at my palm, I touch each smooth surface of the fragile soup bone carvings, miraculously intact throughout generations. My great grandfather, Friedrich Von Schluembach, had whittled three Christian symbols, an anchor, signifying hope, a cross, representing God's love, and a heart, symbolizing faith in God and family. Three charms rendered silky smooth as he fingered each through daily prayer.

Eventually released from Libby Prison, my great grandfather returned to his young wife, Coelestine, raised six children, and became a pastor, The Reverend Friedrich Von Schluembach.

Homemade Vegetable Beef Soup

Passed down through the generations!

Serves 10

Ingredients:

1 medium-size soup bone
2 fatty beef ribs
1 lb. beef for stew
1 tsp. vegetable oil (optional)
1 large onion, thinly sliced
2 (14½-oz.) cans whole tomatoes
6 medium carrots, peeled and sliced about ¼-inch thick
6 medium celery stalks, sliced about ¼-inch thick (no celery leaves)

1 tbsp. salt
¼ tsp. black pepper
1 small bay leaf
4 c. water
1 pkg. frozen chopped green beans (optional)
1 pkg. frozen corn kernels (optional)
¼ c. quick cooking barley (more if desired)
4 fresh parsley sprigs, finely chopped

Directions:

Brown fatty beef ribs and soup bone in a large hot pot or Dutch oven. Turn ribs and soup bone to avoid burning. Remove when browned.

Add stew meat to the remaining hot fat, and brown, turning frequently. Remove meat and reduce heat.

Add 1 teaspoon vegetable oil if needed. Loosen and stir in any browned particles from bottom of pot. Add sliced onions to remaining hot fat or vegetable oil. Brown until transparent, being careful not to burn onions. Once again loosen any browned (not burnt) particles on bottom of pan and stir in.

Add canned tomatoes, carrots, celery, salt, pepper, bay leaf, and 4 cups of water.

Return beef ribs, soup bone, and stew meat to the pot. Simmer 2½ hours.

Frozen vegetables should be added during the last hour of cooking.

Remove soup bone and beef ribs. Pull meat from bones, returning meat only to soup.

Add barley, cooking 30 minutes more.

Before serving, stir in parsley and additional salt and pepper to taste.

—*Ann Kiles McGill*
St. Petersburg, Florida

Legacy of Love and Courage

To me, no food says family like mashed potatoes, and my favorite version comes from my grandmother Lil. Every Thanksgiving, my mother uncovers her battered recipe box and takes out the index card with her mother's recipe. Yellow splotches on the card remind me of my adolescent excitement when my mom finally let me make Lil's recipe—sloppily—on my own.

Lil is ninety-two, and no longer much help in the kitchen. When my grandfather Charlie developed dementia, she stopped taking care of herself because she was afraid to leave him. Years of forgoing doctor's appointments worsened her ailing hip, knee, and eye: self-sacrificial love, borne by her body.

Charlie, and soldiers like him, knew about self-sacrifice. A WWII bombardier, he was shot down, escaped, shot down again, held prisoner in Germany for almost a year, until finally released. Charlie

Charlie and Lil Keck.

told me he was fed thin white mystery gruel. He told me he suffered from dysentery. He told me he saw a guard randomly shoot a fellow prisoner in the head.

Charlie survived the war, but did not survive dementia. Yet thanks to soldiers like Charlie, my family survives to pass down Lil's potato recipe, boiled, thickened with cream cheese, and baked. I hope one day I will make Lil's recipe with my own children, and tell them about their grandfather, who fought evil, almost died, and returned home to meet Lil.

As my children swallow smooth bites of creamy potatoes, I hope they'll remember my grandparents' legacy of courage, and of love.

Baked Whipped Potatoes

Serves 8

Ingredients:
8 medium Idaho potatoes
16 oz. cream cheese
½ small grated onion
2 eggs, beaten
1 tbsp. corn starch
Dash of paprika

*I've modified the original recipe by adding a little bit of chopped garlic, salt, and pepper

Directions:

Boil or microwave potatoes until they are easily pierced by a fork (I've done both peeled and unpeeled, and much prefer the smooth texture of peeled).

Mash potatoes.

Add remaining ingredients and beat to combine.

Bake at 300°F for 45 minutes. About halfway through, remove and stir the potatoes. Sprinkle paprika over top before returning to the oven to finish baking. This really gives it a nice autumnal look.

—Tracy Gold
Writer/Editor/Teacher
Granddaughter of Charles Keck and William Gold, both WWII veterans

Good American Soldier

I confidently predicted two things before watching the almost twenty-year-old interview with my dad, Pete (1921–2004), about his World War II experiences. He would talk about food—and watching the tape he did, but not when I thought he would—and he would be funny—and he was, but he also shed tears, and was reflective in a serious tone.

Why I didn't view this earlier is a mystery of tangled emotions. I've had the tape since a few years after his death. But not until I went to the Armed Forces History Museum in Largo, Florida, and stood before a display case of items from the Army Air Force (the Air Force became its own entity in 1947) did I feel the strength to see and hear this family time capsule.

Revisiting can be painful, but then two things helped me. These were quirks I knew would come across from my gregarious dad. I wanted to see and hear if I was right about the personality I loved so dearly.

Pete entered the service at age twenty-one, very lucky to have had some mechanic training. It probably saved his life because the Army Air Force tested his skills and enrolled him in classes to learn airplane propeller repairs. This kept him somewhat far from battlegrounds for the duration of World War II.

Skip ahead to the end of the war. Pete is transferred to Antwerp, Belgium, from Germany to wait two months for his turn to be shipped home. This is where the food angle would come in, I thought. Belgian chocolate, waffles, and then his daily bus trips to Paris during this time would surely bring mention of croissants and cheese.

But no, the guy who all his life talked incessantly about eating when he wasn't eating saved his food references for the trip home. He fondly recalls the Liberty ship journey back to the USA, because the seas weren't so rough. As the two-week crossing came to a close, the men are "ordered" to eat the ton of ice cream still onboard. "I had to be a good American soldier," beams my dad at the memory.

He says when the Statue of Liberty came into sight, the Army crew rushed to one side to catch a glimpse. My dad worried the ship would tip. "They shouted and screamed and threw everything paper (makeshift confetti) but money overboard."

Pete Jr. eventually took a taxi from the Akron, Ohio, bus station to reunite with my mom, pretty Peg, at their modest apartment. After knocking on the door, he found "someone else there." This is when Dad tears up. The eighteen-month-old Pete III didn't know his dad. So when bedtime later rolled around, the tyke kissed the photograph of the uniformed soldier good night instead of the real thing—now home for good.

During a playful session, Dad tossed his giggly offspring in the air and missed catching him. The crib broke on impact from the heavy toddler. Peg reacted calmly, "Well, I guess that's the way things will be from now on." Happy chaos.

Almost . . . Peg and Pete had another great kid in 1946 and then my little sis in 1950. My siblings both watched the World War II memory lane video many times. I'm grateful I've taken that step now too.

My mother, Peg, was a great cook and baker. When she married my Romanian-heritage dad, Pete, she had to step up to the garlic challenge. He liked it on everything. But since Mom almost fled their first date because of my dad's garlic breath, she had to lessen and lessen its use.

This chicken and dumplings dish is my favorite from my childhood. No garlic; not even using it sparingly. So everyone is happy and kissable!

My mother, Peg Perv. Shreveport, 1943.

My father, Pete Perv. The Romanian name Parvu was changed to Perv when his family landed in Ellis Island. Descendants are in the process of changing the family name back to Parvu.

Pete and Peg in Atlantic City. They stayed at the fancy Clairidge Hotel which was turned over to the military during the war.

Kissable Chicken and Dumplings

Serves 6–8

Ingredients:

3½ lb. frying chicken, cut up into serving portions: breasts, thighs, drumsticks, etc.

2 medium onions, finely chopped

3 tbsp. butter or cooking oil

2 tbsp. chopped fresh parsley

1 tbsp. paprika

1 c. water

Salt and pepper

Directions:

The day before making, cut up chicken, wash, dry, and sprinkle with salt, then place in covered bowl in refrigerator overnight.

Sauté onions in butter or oil, then add chicken and brown slightly on each side.

Add parsley, paprika, and water.

Simmer for 45 minutes or until chicken is tender (this is the total cooking time, you add the dumplings the last 20 minutes before chicken is done). Add salt and pepper to taste.

Authors' note: *You may want to debone and remove skin before dumplings are added.*

Dumplings

Ingredients:

3 eggs

1 tbsp. water

¼ tsp. salt

Unbleached flour (start with ¾ cup, keep adding until right consistency)

Directions:

Slightly beat eggs, water, and salt together.

Add flour gradually until batter is of the consistency to drop slowly off a spoon.

Drop by tablespoons into lightly salted boiling water and simmer 25 minutes.

Drain through slotted spoon and add to chicken for the last 20 minutes of its cooking time.

Enjoy this cozy dish!

—*Janis D. Froelich*
Graduate of Kent State University, worked for five newspapers during her forty-year journalism career: Kent Record-Courier, Akron Beacon Journal, Tampa Bay Times, Des Moines Register *and* Tampa Tribune. *She lives on Tierra Verde, Florida, and attends writing classes at Eckerd College's OLLI program.*

Military Service: A Family Tradition

My mother, Letha Warren Hogg, was the middle child of seven. She had one sister and five brothers.

They grew up in an oil-boom town in south Arkansas where their father worked at the Lion Oil refinery. Their mother died when my mother was seven years old and they were raised by housekeepers and a stepmother. But they grew up with a sense of pride in being an American, and a patriotic sense of duty.

When World War II broke out, four of her siblings joined the military, while Mother did her part to support the war effort at home. Her sister, Lucretia, joined the Navy as a WAVE and at age ninety still relates the story of being one of the pinup girls and has the pictures to prove it.

William, the oldest, joined the Marines and tragically died in a car accident while stationed in Hawaii. Alfred joined the Army and served in the 101st Airborne during WWII and Korea, and was often accused of being crazy for jumping out of a perfectly good airplane. In today's service, he would be diagnosed with PTSD. J. W. joined the Air Force, and Joe joined the Navy. Wayne, who was much younger than his brothers, opted to join the National Guard.

William, Alfred, J. W., and Joe all made the military a career and retired after twenty-plus years of service.

After the war, the brothers were stationed all over the world. I cannot remember any time during my childhood when all of the siblings were gathered in one place at one time. But they each came home for periodic visits when they had leave. Most of the visits were during one holiday or another and they always wanted Mother's cornbread dressing with giblet gravy.

We sometimes had Christmas in July when it came to meals. Although my mother is no longer with us, we are carrying on the tradition at Thanksgiving with her cornbread dressing and giblet gravy.

Cornbread Dressing

Serves 16–20

Ingredients:

2 whole chickens + 3 chicken bouillon cubes, covered with water then simmered until juices run clear (about 1 hour), or pressure cooked, or 2 store-bought rotisserie chickens

3 lbs cornbread, crumbled

2 large onions, chopped

2 celery stalks finely, chopped

2 slices light bread, broken up

Pepper and Poultry Seasoning to taste

12 eggs, lightly beaten

Directions:

Debone and chop or shred cooked chicken into bite-size pieces. Measure out 2–3 cups of chicken for this recipe, and reserve the rest for another use. Set aside the cooking broth.

Combine your 2–3 cups chicken with the remaining ingredients.

Turn into large oven-safe pan.

Add enough of the reserved broth to moisten, but not make soggy.

Bake at 350°F until done (approximately 1 hour).

Giblet Gravy

Ingredients:

Giblets from turkey or chicken

4 tbsp. of unbaked cornbread dressing

4 c. reserved chicken broth

1–3 tbsp. cornstarch

1 hard-boiled egg (coarsely chopped)

Salt and pepper

Directions:

In a medium-sized saucepan, place giblets in enough water to cover. Gently boil until tender. Remove and cut up giblets.

Add enough chicken broth to the giblet cooking water to make 4 cups. Add cornstarch 1 tablespoon at a time to thicken.

Add remaining ingredients and the cut-up giblets.

Cook over low to medium heat until desired consistency; stirring occasionally.

—Linda Hogg Mandell
Daughter of Letha Warren Hogg

Celebrity Heroes

I'm not one to dote on celebrities. I don't buy *InStyle* or follow the Kardashians, wouldn't recognize Justin Bieber if he sat next to me, or pretend to know who is on the current Hollywood "A" list. I know for some, they serve as an outlet from the humdrum of everyday life, to admire, respect, or sometimes vilify, and that is fine—just not for me.

The exception are those celebrities who use their fame to further causes dear to my heart, namely our military heroes. I wrote to Robert Irvine, asking him to share a special recipe for this book. I was honored and delighted when he agreed.

Not only is Chef Irvine the star of several popular television shows, but he also started a foundation to raise funds

Chef Robert Irvine.

for military veterans: The Robert Irvine Foundation. He is a veteran of the Royal Navy, and an honorary Chief Petty Officer of the US Navy. He has rescued restaurants, cooked for presidents, written several books on healthy eating, and is an outstanding role model for healthy living.

Thank you, Chef Irvine, for all you do.

—*Tracey Enerson Wood*
St. Petersburg, FL

Braised Beef Short Ribs

Serves 4

Ingredients:

Beef short ribs, about 4 lb., cut English style
    (cut between the bones into thick chunks)

Cure

1 tbsp. kosher salt
1 tsp. TCM* (optional)
1 tsp. black pepper

Braising Liquid

2 carrots
1 whole onion
2 ribs celery
1 qt. red wine
2 qts. beef stock (chicken stock a suitable
    substitute)

Sachet

4 bay leaves
4 sprigs thyme
2 sprigs rosemary
1 tbsp. peppercorns
1 tsp. whole allspice

Directions:

Combine all the ingredients for the cure and rub on the ribs thoroughly.

Allow the ribs to cure under refrigeration for around 12 hours. If you don't have 12 hours, a 4–6 hour cure is also okay.

Remove the ribs from the cooler and sear in a roasting pan over medium high heat on the stove. Be sure to sear the ribs on all sides to get a fair amount of color.

While the ribs are cooking, large dice the carrots, onions, and celery.

Prepare the sachet*.

Once all of the ribs have been seared, turn the heat down to medium and add the carrots, celery, and onions (mire poix).

Cook the mire poix until it has softened and has taken on some color; this should take about 20–25 minutes.

Remove the ribs, and with the vegetables still in the pan, add the red wine and deglaze. Turn the heat up to high and be sure to remove any fond* stuck to the bottom of the pan. Once the wine has almost completely reduced, add the beef stock.

Add the beef ribs back to the pan, cover completely with water, and add your sachet. If the ribs do not fit in the roaster completely covered with braising liquid, place in to two smaller vessels.

Bring the roasting pan back to a simmer, and cover with parchment first and then tin foil on top.

Place in the oven to braise for 5 hours at 250°F, check to make sure the ribs are done before removing from the oven. If necessary, continue to cook, checking periodically until the meat begins to fall off the bone.

Authors' Notes:

*TCM is Tinted Cure Mix, also known as Prague Powder 1. It is a salt mixture, tinted pink for identification, used for curing and preserving meat. It is available on Amazon or specialty food outlets. It helps speed the curing process, but is optional in this recipe.

*Fond, French for "base," refers to the browned bits and caramelized drippings of meat and vegetables stuck to the bottom of the pan after roasting.

*To make a sachet, bundle the herbs and spices into a small square of cheesecloth and secure with butcher's string.

—Robert Irvine
Celebrity Chef, Entrepreneur, Philanthropist, and Founder of the Robert Irvine Foundation
Host of Food Network's "Restaurant: Impossible" and "Dinner: Impossible"

Piggy Bank Promises

The piggy bank was a much admired artifact that sat on the oak floor of Frank and Jewell Enerson's apartment in Rutherford, New Jersey. It was the late 1950s, and there was at least a half dozen of us grandkids by then. On Sunday afternoons, we would gather for Grandma's scrumptious roast beef dinners. Afterwards, we'd crawl up to the heavy molded-chalk piggy bank and surround it, amazed how heavy it was from being stuffed with all those coins! We challenged each other to lift it off the living room floor.

I remember fussing at Grandma one day, repeatedly asking, "Grandma, Grandma, what are you going to do with all that money?"

She would always reply, looking us straight in the eyes, "That money is for your college education."

I remember quietly thinking, *Wow! I'm going to college!*

Expectations were set. Our grandparents were the children of immigrants, and a college education was not possible for them. But their three sons went to college on the G.I. Bill, and their daughter attended a hospital school of nursing. The next generation was expected to follow suit—no, to surpass the achievements of the previous generation.

On August 1, 1966, Grandpa Frank Enerson passed away at seventy years old. We speculated that his kidneys failed from all the "Tums" and antacids he ate for forty years. His heartburn always made him grouchy, but Grandma always adored and fussed over him. We couldn't imagine what she would do without him.

Shortly after Grandpa passed, Grandma moved to a smaller apartment nearby. Money was tight. We were all upset about her moving; we loved her old apartment. It sat on the banks of the Passaic River, and had a great lawn with a view. I remember watching in amazement as the nearby Union Avenue Bridge would ring its bells and open up to let ships and barges pass by. It was a neat spot.

Shortly after her move, we all congregated in her new space on a fall Sunday. Roast beef dinner was replaced with sandwiches and cookies, but we didn't care. I was excited to tell Grandma about my first weeks as a freshman in high school. She was pleased but I could sense her anguish with all the changes occurring in her life.

My brothers, sisters, and cousins checked out her new apartment, not so excited, missing the old place. It was smaller and seemed simple. We gathered on the living room floor, surrounding the old piggy bank, like old times.

My brother picked up the piggy bank with surprising ease. He raised it in the air and we could see that it was empty! It had a crack on its side and the bottom was opened. We stared, bug-eyed, our mouths gaping open.

I saw Grandma watching us from across the room. She turned, walked away, and held her face. She was crying into her hands. My father noticed too and chased after her into the small kitchen. I followed.

My dad held her as she covered her face, crying over the kitchen sink. "Mom, Mom, what's wrong?" he asked.

Jewell Cusack Enerson was a smart, strong, experienced New York Irish woman. Her brother was killed in WWI, she successfully raised four children in the Depression, then sent all three of her sons off to World War II and its aftermath, and in support of the Korean War. She was not an overly emotional woman, but a kind and strong wife and mother. I don't think I ever saw her cry before this day.

Dad was holding her with his chest to her back. "Mom, what's wrong?" he asked again.

She sobbed, and finally replied, "I had to empty the piggy bank. How do I explain this— that money was for them. I'm so ashamed."

He held her and rocked her slowly. "You have nothing to be ashamed of, nothing," he said as he continued to comfort her. She turned, facing him as she wiped her face. "Those kids love you, and, they know that you love them, that's all that matters," he told her, holding her tightly.

She nodded her head, found a tissue from her apron pocket and dabbed at her tears. "I know, I know. That's what matters."

Grandma and her piggy bank worked! All five of my brothers and sisters and I graduated college!

—*Bob Enerson*
Richmond, VA

Sunday Dinner Roast Beef

Sunday dinner at my grandparents' was always roast beef. My grandmother's cooking was typical of those days with no fussy steps or ingredients. I don't know what cut of beef my grandmother used, but I prefer silver tip. It's a leaner cut and I always have my butcher lard and tie it.

Serves 6 with enough for leftovers for roast beef sandwiches

Ingredients:
1 Silver Tip roast, larded & tied, about 3.5 lb.
Montreal steak seasoning
½ c. red wine or beef stock

Directions:

Heat oven to 350°F.

Take roast out of fridge and let it come to room temperature (45-60 minutes).

Season on all sides with Montreal steak seasoning. Put in shallow baking pan (about 2 inches) and roast for 70 minutes (20 minutes per pound).

Ten minutes before removing from the oven, add red wine or beef stock to the pan.

Remove roast from oven, tent with foil, and let rest 15 minutes. Slice and serve with pan juice.

Chef's Note: Roast will be rare. Warm sliced beef to your preferred taste. Leftover suggestion: Roast beef sandwich with horseradish-bacon mayo, Swiss cheese, lettuce, and tomato on toasted rye.

Author's note: *I use a meat thermometer, and remove from oven at 125ºF.*

Chef Julia Enerson
Julia's Greek Kitchen
juliamenerson@gmail.com
Fair Lawn, NJ

Grandma's Chicken-N-Dumplings

This was the one dish my husband, Scott, always wanted after a long TDY (temporary duty) or deployment. His idea of quintessential home cooking: the comfort of home, the taste of home. Use cast iron Dutch oven.

Serves 4

Ingredients:

2½ lb. fryer chicken
2–3 carrots, sliced
2–3 celery stalks, sliced
1 onion, diced
Fresh parsley, chopped
4 c. water
Chicken bouillon

3 tbsp. corn starch
1 c. milk
Salt and pepper

For Dumplings:
2 c. biscuit mix (tested with Bisquik)
⅔ c. milk

Directions:

Wash chicken, remove any parts packed inside. Place in pot with carrots, celery, and onion. Add parsley, pinch of salt, and ground pepper as desired. Cover ingredients with water and add appropriate amount of chicken bouillon.

Cook on stove for approximately 1 hour.

When chicken is tender, remove from broth and cool. Debone chicken.

Mix corn starch and milk. Add to chicken broth and bring back to boil. Stir while simmering for 15 minutes (broth will thicken to gravy). Add salt and pepper to taste.

Return chicken to broth/gravy and continue to simmer while preparing biscuit dumplings.

Dumplings:

Using a fork, mix biscuit mix and milk until soft dough forms.

Drop spoonfuls on top of gravy (start by making outer ring of dumplings along pot edge).

While gravy is simmering, cook dumplings for 10 minutes, uncovered,

Continue cooking, covered, for 10 minutes (raising lid can cause dumplings to be tough).

—Julia Martin
Eagle River, Alaska

USS Ronald Reagan homecoming, 2006.

FINAL THOUGHTS
Musings on Life and Military Service

D-Day

In 2007 I met Bill, an eighty-two year-old ex-paratrooper, at a gymnasium where we both worked on fitness. He jumped with the 101st Airborne on D-Day as a private in the 377th Parachute Field Artillery Battalion. He was a five-foot-eight-inch, balding, voluble, physically fit, and friendly man with a Brooklyn accent. My daughter Janna, and her husband, Rusty, an army veteran, were visiting us and joined me on the interview with Bill at his favorite joint in his neighborhood, "El Cap." After lunch, we went to his nearby home to talk and see his memorabilia stored in a small room in a neat, sixty-year-old house.

Born and raised in New York City, he joined the army at age eighteen. Trained at Fort Benning with six jumps before going by convoy transport to Liverpool, he then further trained in the English countryside with night jumps.

Bill had a few scrapes. He went *AWOL* (absent without leave) for a few nights when stuck in a port at Greenland for ship repairs. He and a pal would slip out of a port hole and go visit the girls at night, until he was caught and placed in the brig. On his first night jump, he hit a tree and spent a few days in the hospital. He enjoyed his stay in England.

On D-Day, he landed twelve miles away from Carenten, their objective. Landing on a German bunker, he could see the English Channel. When a German came out to look at him, Bill "played dead" as the German raised Bill's helmet up with a rifle barrel. He said, "I was always captured on training maneuvers in the states, so I knew just what to do."

When the German went back into the bunker, Bill threw a grenade into the gun slit and "got out of there in a hurry—we were told not to perform individual feats like that."

Bill then wandered around in a mine field until daylight, when he discovered his dilemma. Two days later, he and twenty-five others came back and killed or captured 135 enemy troops. Most were Poles or east Europeans with SS officers in charge of them.

In September, his outfit jumped into Holland and twelve weeks later, in December, were rushed to Belgium in open trucks to reinforce the Battle of the Bulge. While in Bastogne he learned that his older brother was nearby with Patton's tank division. Bill stole a jeep belonging to General McCullough and found his brother. They celebrated by knocking on local citizens' doors to see if they had any wine or beer. Unknown to them, the back of the jeep was full of whiskey. He did not share the consequences of his *AWOL* and theft. His brother survived the war and died a few years ago.

Bill had a photo album of war scenes: bunkers, disabled German tanks and artillery, many of his buddies, dead soldiers (Americans and Germans) laid out for burial in a field. Cameras were not allowed, but one of Bill's friends found a German camera with film and took these pictures, and later had given Bill copies.

Bill is now losing his memory on current events, but his past memories seem very good. He enjoyed telling his story, although he would become sad talking about the friends he had lost in the war.

Bill's past has become his daily life: going to the restaurant, working out at the gym, and seeing friends at the VFW hall. "My wife doesn't know I go to the VFW so much, but I take off my jacket and leave it in the car before I go into the VFW, so the smoke won't be on my clothing."

Bill was mustered out at a ski resort in Austria. He had received many ribbons and medals, but regrets not getting a Purple Heart, although he had pneumonia and frostbite requiring hospitalization in Belgium. He came back to the United States, and worked as an engineer for the city of New York, maintaining water lines. He had jumped with other paratroopers on anniversaries in Holland and Normandy. During the 50th anniversary of D-Day, the government would not sanction a commemorative jump, so through a benefactor, they leased a plane and a field and made a jump anyway. His last jump in Normandy was in 2004, when he was seventy-nine years old. His daughter would not let him jump anymore, but he felt quite safe in his hobby.

—Bill Priest, as told to
James Endicott,
St. Petersburg, FL

Survival Skills and the Amorous Moose

My grandfather, Alfred Wood, was born on December 2, 1896, in West Yorkshire, England, and was orphaned at the age of seven. Due to the family's desperate financial situation, British officials sent him to Ontario, Canada, where he served as a farm laborer in numerous homes, attending "home school," which was mostly working in the fields and learning on his own.

In 1914, my grandfather escaped the abusive foster homes by enlisting in the Canadian Infantry, deploying to Belgium during WWI. He fought in the trenches for three-plus years, in the most oppressive, unimaginable combat conditions. Wounded twice, he was also exposed to mustard gas during two separate attacks, nearly killing him during the battles of Ypres and Passchendaele. If the enemy didn't kill them, disease and exposure would—Alfred was one of six soldiers to return home from his company of 150.

Upon return to Canada, he kept in touch with his Canadian Army buddies during hunts in the Nipigon Ontario region. Capitalizing on the excellent marksmanship skills he learned in combat, moose-hunting provided much needed protein for his family during and after the Great Depression. Even after immigrating to Ohio prior to WWII, Alfred kept in touch with his buddies through the annual hunts and relished the comradery with his former battle mates.

During one of these hunts in early September, the group set up camp at the edge of a lake. The next morning, they set out in canoes. There were no moose sightings during the first couple of days of swapping war stories while shivering in leaky canoes.

Alfred developed a bad cold with a rather raspy cough. His buddies informed him it would be best for him to stay in camp, rest, and prepare their dinner after they returned from a hard day of hunting. Feeling somewhat dejected at being designated "rear echelon" for the day, Alfred began taking care of routine camp chores in preparation for dinner, interrupted by frequent bouts of uncontrollable coughing.

After one of the coughing spells, he heard a series of grunts from the nearby wood line: "umph, umph, umph," in a rhythmic pattern. Another series of coughs was answered by higher paced, more synchronized, and closer series of grunts. This (cough) call and answer was repeated a few times, until antlers appeared thrashing through the brush.

A large bull moose, in full rut, was heading to camp, looking for the cow moose in heat. My grandfather grabbed his .270 Winchester rifle in self-defense. At twenty yards, with no sign of the bull moose slowing down, Alfred shot, and the moose dropped at the edge of camp.

Hearing the gunfire, the rest of the hunting party returned to camp to discover the designated non-hunting cook was the only hunter to get a moose. Dinner around the campfire was particularly memorable that night, after a tough day of hunting and butchering a 1200+ pound animal. Moose tenderloin was on the menu, and my grandfather was the proud provider for his fellow veterans.

The bull moose antlers were proudly displayed above the garage, so all and any curious passersby could be treated to a lively retelling of the adventure. Grandpa passed down to me the .270 Winchester, a most useful and cherished heirloom, which I will someday hand down to my son. My grandmother Maude was an excellent cook, and I remember her preparing moose for our family dinners. The distinguishing feature of this dish was her rich, dark gravy, which made the meal.

—Dave Wood
COL (Ret.) US Army
Grandson of WWI Canadian Army Veteran
Son of WWII US Navy Veteran
Father of US Army Active Duty Officer
Father-in-law of US Navy Active Duty Officer

Polish Pottery and the Military

As we packed up for yet another move (for the twenty-first time during my husband's career), a friend on the Army post came by with a good-bye gift. It was a stars and stripes pattern coffee mug of the Polish Pottery style, which is so popular with military families. My friend was astounded that I had never collected Polish Pottery in my husband's thirty-two-year career but wanted to get me started. I vowed to use her gift every day.

Later, after moving into our first home in the civilian world for our retirement assignment, I bought a fairly expensive set of dishes as a sort of celebration and used them every day. Hardly a year had gone by and every single piece had a chip in it. It was maddening!

However, true to my word, I also used that Polish Pottery coffee mug every single day and that thing was a tank. Not a chip. I still have it a decade later, and nary a scratch. So, I caved after all those years and started collecting Polish Pottery, just as so many other military families had.

That was the beginning of my love affair with the versatile and delightfully sturdy world of Polish Pottery. It is why you'll see it on many of these pages, as it is a familiar staple on military dinner tables. The patterns don't need to match, they are inexpensive, pack very well, and can stand up to the rigors of frequent moves—the perfect set of dishes for military families.

—Carol Van Drie
Okemos, MI

Controlled Application

Oh yes, that was my business.
The controlled application of violence.

With instruments that were not gentle or soft or comforting.
Instead they were swift and cruel and cared nothing for fairness or friendship.

That was long ago and now I am somebody else.
Somebody less rigid.
Somebody less firm.
Somebody less detached and cold.

It doesn't work.
My former self won't lie down, but now I'm empty handed.
Like "air guitar" and I can't stop playing.

—David Washechek
Katy, TX
COL, US Army (Ret.)

The last letter sent by Pvt. Timothy Cusack, October 26, 1918

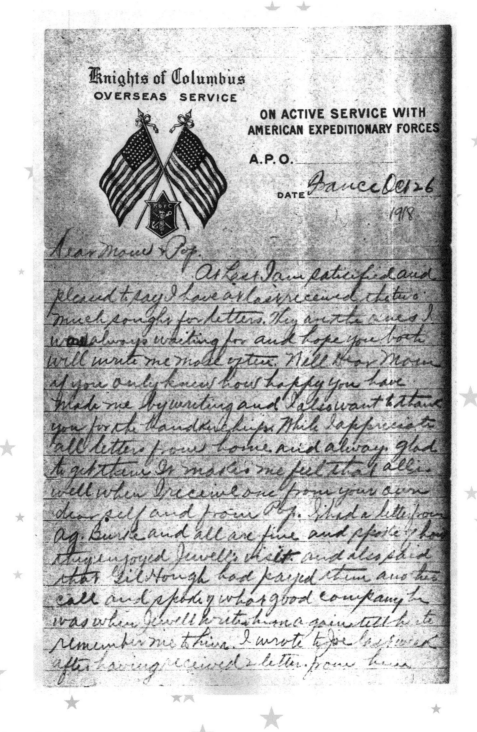

and explained why the long delays in not writing sooner. But we have little or nothing for ourselves and seldom we can write because when we move no mail can be taken from us unless we are settled for at least a few days, and that has not been very often since July, so you can easily see how we are handicapped as far as writing is concerned. But with all this inconvienence I can safely say I am feeling fine and strong and am still good for a stiff tussle if it has to come. I am glad to hear about the way the people back home acting. Well Pop keep on building them ships because if we can believe half of the rumors we hear we will need them to carry us home some time next spring and it cant come to quick for any of us over here because all the boys are just as anxious to get home as you are to greet us. So for that reason we all must be patient and wait. I had a letter from Matt also so I suppose he told you what he wrote me about his being called + near deaf. While I think of it I want to mention that I have not received the package Florence sent me as yet. But they all seem to be slow in coming so I guess I will get mine when my turn comes. The packages that are received are nothing wonderful and most of time sending only things from home.

Knights of Columbus
OVERSEAS SERVICE

**ON ACTIVE SERVICE WITH
AMERICAN EXPEDITIONARY FORCES**

A.P.O.

DATE

We were treated to another divisional show
here and met Jack McNulty there he looks
good getting plenty of Vin Blanc (wine) and
he asks to be remembered to all at home. He
told me about Mike Twinlaw being over and
that he was in Division Hd. qrts. stationed
in a big city lucky Mike. Also met Eddie
Arvie. he also looks good and was asking to
be remembered to all. We had open service
and received absolution and expect to
receive Holy Communion to-morrow.
Just to let you know that I am not neglecting
my religion. I attend whenever possible
so you can rest easy as far as that's concerned.
Well folks I guess I will say good night. Hoping
all at home are in good health and that all
of us, with lots of love and kisses for all with
hopes of more mail I am Lovingly
Ted H.

Private H. Cisco 16 Co. K. 30 Inf

Note from the Authors

Requesting, collecting, reading, and editing these stories and recipes has been a challenge, a joy, and heartbreaking, sometimes all at the same time. Meeting the veterans and their loved ones, whether in person, online, or through the mail, has been a reward beyond measure. It is truly a privilege to preserve their family histories in this way.

Although this is a work of nonfiction, the authors do not claim to have verified the stories presented by our many contributors. Details in family lore often become twisted through generations of re-telling. We encourage readers to accept the stories as true as far as the teller knows, and to enjoy the spirit and meaningfulness within them.

From left to right: Tracey Enerson Wood, Beth Guidry Riffle, and Carol Van Drie.

Acknowledgments

Writing, or in truth, collecting this book has been more a calling than an inspiration. The idea came to me while musing the intricacies and difficulties in writing and marketing historical novels. I wondered, *what stories need to be told? What stories do we need to hear; what voices must be preserved, before they are lost forever?*

I thought about my many friends and family members who are veterans, and possessed memories about their service, or about their ancestors' service, that were important tidbits of American history—anecdotes that would never make history books, or films, or journals. Bits and pieces from lives spent in service, which would surely fade away with time. Rather than fictionalize, I felt an unworldly persuasion to collect them in their own voices, from their own memories. So, I acknowledge a higher power that led me on this journey.

I'd like to sincerely thank all those that shared this dream of preserving this slice of Americana, all the contributors of stories, recipes, photos, and ideas. Most especially, I'd like to thank my husband, Dave Wood, for his unending love and patience with me; my editor, Leah Zarra, and the entire Skyhorse team; my agent, Lucy Cleland, for her early support even before a story had been written; my co-authors/dear friends/family: Carol Van Drie and Beth Riffle; my beloved kids: Kristen Riffle and Erik Wood, and their own wonderful, beautiful families. My eternal gratitude to professional photographers Grab Szenas and Steve Dean, and designer Diane Phelps, all who devoted more time and effort than I could possibly afford; Pat Brown and the entire Eckerd College Olli Writing Circle; Tom Cuba, Jami Diese, Ann Hood, Robert Irvine, Antigone Doucette, the PitchWars class of 2015, all who wrote stories, or cheered me on and were always there for me. God bless our veterans and their loved ones.

—*Tracey Enerson Wood*
January, 2018
St. Petersburg, FL

Index

Conversion Charts

Metric and Imperial Conversions
(These conversions are rounded for convenience)

Ingredient	Cups/ Tablespoons/ Teaspoons	Ounces	Grams/Milliliters
Butter	1 cup/ 16 tablespoons/ 2 sticks	8 ounces	230 grams
Cheese, shredded	1 cup	4 ounces	110 grams
Cream cheese	1 tablespoon	0.5 ounce	14.5 grams
Cornstarch	1 tablespoon	0.3 ounce	8 grams
Flour, all-purpose	1 cup/1 tablespoon	4.5 ounces/0.3 ounce	125 grams/8 grams
Flour, whole wheat	1 cup	4 ounces	120 grams
Fruit, dried	1 cup	4 ounces	120 grams
Fruits or veggies, chopped	1 cup	5 to 7 ounces	145 to 200 grams
Fruits or veggies, puréed	1 cup	8.5 ounces	245 grams
Honey, maple syrup, or corn syrup	1 tablespoon	.75 ounce	20 grams
Liquids: cream, milk, water, or juice	1 cup	8 fluid ounces	240 milliliters
Oats	1 cup	5.5 ounces	150 grams
Salt	1 teaspoon	0.2 ounces	6 grams
Spices: cinnamon, cloves, ginger, or nutmeg (ground)	1 teaspoon	0.2 ounce	5 milliliters
Sugar, brown, firmly packed	1 cup	7 ounces	200 grams
Sugar, white	1 cup/1 tablespoon	7 ounces/0.5 ounce	200 grams/12.5 grams
Vanilla extract	1 teaspoon	0.2 ounce	4 grams

Oven Temperatures

Fahrenheit	Celsius	Gas Mark
225°	110°	¼
250°	120°	½
275°	140°	1
300°	150°	2
325°	160°	3
350°	180°	4
375°	190°	5
400°	200°	6
425°	220°	7
450°	230°	8